EGYPT
THE ETERNAL SMILE

EGYPT
THE ETERNAL SMILE

REFLECTIONS ON A JOURNEY
BY ALLEN DRURY
PHOTOGRAPHED BY ALEX GOTFRYD

DOUBLEDAY & COMPANY, INC., GARDEN CITY, NEW YORK, 1980

ISBN 0-385-00193-2
LIBRARY OF CONGRESS CATALOG CARD NUMBER 78-20069
TEXT COPYRIGHT © 1980 BY ALLEN DRURY
PHOTOGRAPHS COPYRIGHT © 1980 BY ALEX GOTFRYD
ALL RIGHTS RESERVED
PRINTED IN THE UNITED STATES OF AMERICA
FIRST EDITION

DEDICATED
TO
THE LATE
JAMES H. BREASTED

The more books one reads on Egypt,
the more one concludes that this pioneer Egyptologist,
while overruled on some points by later research, was,
and overall remains, the best.

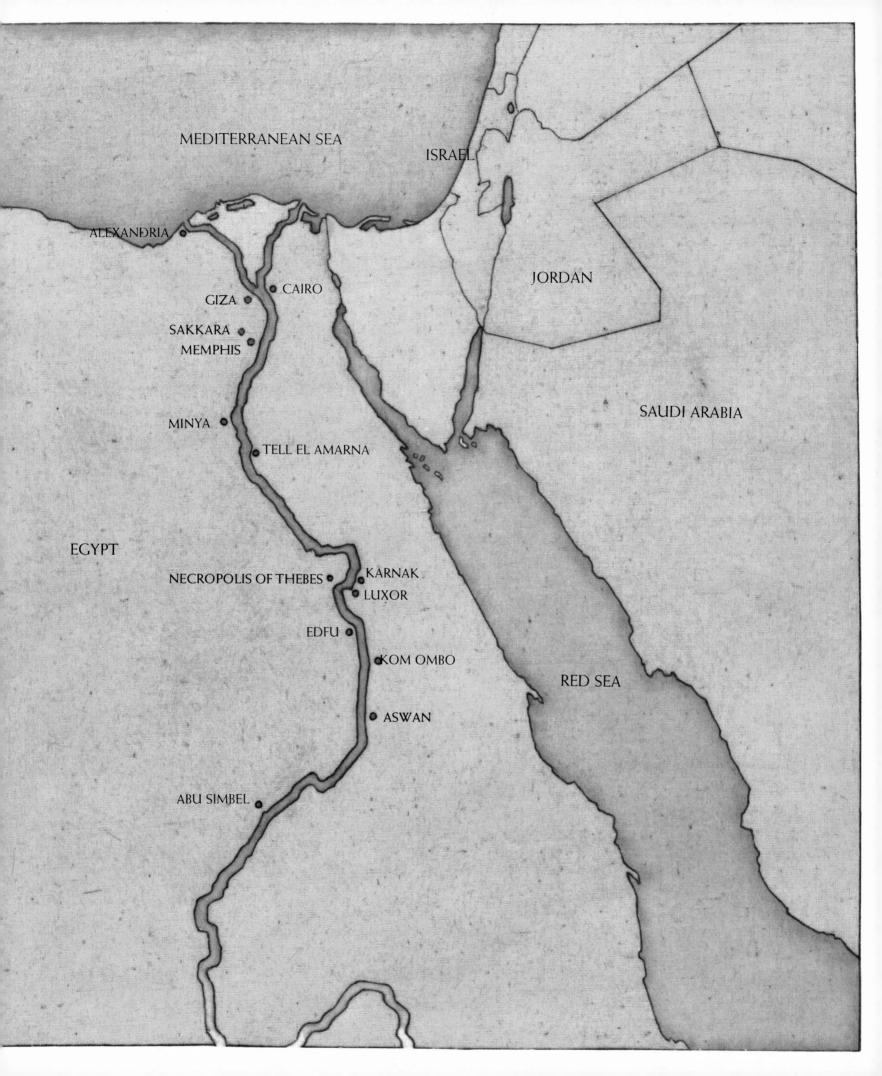

A Note on Narration

For hieroglyphic texts three thousand, sometimes five thousand years in the public domain—which is exactly where the pharaohs intended them to be—I have generally followed the translations of Drs. James H. Breasted, Adolf Erman, Sir Alan Gardiner, Barbara Mertz and Joseph Kaster, now and then changing or substituting a word or phrase that seems better suited. In true pharaonic fashion, I make no apologies for this. Each translator has brought his or her vocabulary, his or her best guess as to what the Ancient Egyptians meant, to the rendering. Many words and phrases are sheer happenstance based upon the education, etymology and background of the translator. Frequently they differ sharply from one another, leading to endless agreements, disagreements, footnotes and argumentative asides. I have dispensed with all this. Where a word has the same general sense but sounds better or more logical to my ear, I have put it in. I doubt that any honest Egyptologist will really quarrel very hard with this.

One thing I have consciously tried to do, and that is steer away from the endless thee-ing and thou-ing which is only an echo of the Bible and in no way indigenous to an Egypt millennia before it.

Ancient Egyptian names are difficult, but not all that difficult. Anyone with half an ear and the patience to sound them out phonetically can arrive at an easy approximation very quickly. I have followed the practice of syllabifying each name on first mention, using it unbroken thereafter, i.e., Amon-ho-tep, Amonhotep.

The name of the sun-god varies with the individual scholar, some preferring Re, pronounced "Ray" or "Reh." This seems to me awkward to the Western tongue and I have called him Ra, pronounced "Rah," throughout, both when standing alone and in royal names such as Se-ke-nen-Ra, Khaf-Ra, and the like. Similarly with the god Amon, who appears variously as Amon, Amun and Amen. For simplicity and consistency's sake he is Amon to me, both when standing alone and in such names as Amon-em-het, Tut-ankh-Amon and Amon-Ra.

Here, again, difficulties began with the original translators. Ancient Egypt had a hieroglyphic "alphabet" that had no vowels. Amon was written approximately "Mn." It is again sheer happenstance that the first people coming across this, who arbitrarily inserted vowels because they could not conceive of pronouncing or writing words without them, did not christen him "Emen," "Imin," "Omon," "Umun," or even "Amin," as in Idi. Fortunately, because we are now used to it, they decided on an "A" to start him off with; but, being an arbitrary choice, it could easily have been any one of the four other vowels. This also gives one substantial leeway in the treatment of proper names and geographic sites. Here too I have opted for the spelling easiest on eye, ear and tongue.

I have generally followed the route of the journey taken by myself, photographer Alex Gotfryd and aide-de-trip Bill Howard Eichstadt as a framework on which to hang the text. It has provided a handy vantage-point from which to comment on Egypt both ancient and modern. Aside from a few annoying but minor problems along the way, the venture went very well. It was also fun. With luck, some of this will have transmitted itself to the text.

Allen Drury

EGYPT
THE ETERNAL SMILE

"And how," inquired the beautiful lady in Luxor with a studied brightness, "will your book about Egypt differ from all the others?"

To this there were two possible answers.

The flippant:

"Madame, we have discovered twenty new tombs in the Valley of the Kings and we are going to publish our findings to an astounded world."

The pertinent:

"Madame, if every author were asked a similar question as he is about to begin a book, no more books would ever be written about anything."

We were there to see Egypt our way, to present our conclusions, to offer our prisms through which to view both the still-powerful mystique of the Ancients and the surge of modern Egypt. We were not there to be different from all the others, except as we were different from all the others. We needed no excuse, though challenged to give one. Manners prevented the tart retort; the conversation trailed away in a mixture of vodka and French. We continued on our way, completed our work, departed Egypt with its secret—if there is one—locked inside us, to be divulged in due time to the astounded world.

Only as we were different would our product be different. And we were a little different from other visitors: somewhere between the solitary red-faced Britisher of the eighteen hundreds—puffing his lonely way with native bearer or two through marsh and sedge to find the secrets of the bloody Nile—and the cattle-loads of Germans, French, Americans, British, roaring into Cairo on the jets, jamming into buses, swarming the tombs and temples in hot, exhausted, mind-blurred thousands who dimly grasp and swiftly forget the jumble of history and statistics flung at them by guides who vary greatly in skill, intelligence and devotion to their jobs.

Many helped. Dr. Shehata Adam, president of the Organization of Antiquities, opened many doors for us along the Nile. Dr. James Allen, young, enthusiastic, invaluably helpful director of the American Research Center in Egypt, could not have been more cooperative, encouraging and supportive. Dr. Kent Weeks of the University of California at Berkeley, head of a team that is doing a definitive mapping of the tombs in the Valley of the Kings for the Egyptian Government, furnished many names and suggestions. Dr. David Silverman, now of the University of Pennsylvania, formerly with the Oriental Institute in Chicago, also helped with many suggestions. Officials of the magnificent hodgepodge that is the Cairo Museum—magnificent, and also, due to a lack of funds that is no fault of theirs or their government's, magnificently dirty, dusty and disorganized. Officials of the small, gem-like, totally different and totally effective Luxor Museum. Local directors of antiquities, rousing themselves in the sometimes oppressive heat of Upper Egypt to take the foreign visitors where they wanted to go, invariably patient, good-natured and helpful.

And many, many ordinary Egyptians, taxi drivers, felucca boat pilots, hardworking fellahin in the fields, children waving along the roadside, children begging in the villages, fast-talking men and boys who swarm around the tourists at the monuments pulling made-yesterday antiques from the folds of their flowing white gelabayas... all of these contributed to an understanding of Egypt, as they do for most perceptive visitors, though the past, of course, contributes more... everywhere present, everywhere under the surface of things: most overwhelming and impressive in the Sphinx and Pyramids at Giza and the Old Kingdom burial ground at Sakkara, both near Cairo—at desolate Abu Simbel, far up the Nile—at lonely Tell el-Amarna, capital of doomed Akh-en-aten and beautiful Ne-fer-ti-ti, halfway down the river—above all at Luxor, ancient Thebes, seat of most of the greatest pharaohs, haunt of most of the greatest gods.

We traveled on our own, armed with passes and cameras and, in two cases, previous memories to match the trip against. Some Cairo hotelkeepers and taxicab drivers had grown worse, getting conditioned to cheat by the enormous and steadily growing influx of visitors. But new hotels are being built, and soon the room shortage will not be so great, and hoteliers rude and arrogant now will eat a little humbler pie when competition forces them to. And the taxidrivers who cheat still have what some of the hoteliers have lost in their greed for the tourist coin—that underlying, spontaneous, unconquerable Egyptian charm that bounces back with a laugh and a shrug when the cheater is fairly caught. It has always been a buyer-beware part of the world—that's the fun of the game. They try it on for size, asking two pounds from the Hilton to the great bazaar of Khan el-Khalili, but the minute after you have got them down to one pound, or sometimes lower, they are chatting cheerfully as with old friends, no grudges held. Some other tourist, new to the country and not so knowledgeable, will come along soon. It will all balance out.

Indeed, most things in Egypt do balance out, even today. Wherever she is now—and it seems fair to think she is still somewhere about—the goddess Ma'at, goddess of balance—justice—*the way things were in the beginning—the way they should be maintained always*—is looking on with a smile. Her children are still a pleasant race. They are much changed now from the ones she knew, mixed with the blood of many invaders, yet still, after five millennia, able to produce, on a crowded Cairo street, or waving from a cotton field, or strolling the riverbank at Luxor, startling faces that seem to have come straight off the temple walls, as ancient-looking now as they were then.

And in their hearts, their ways, their daily living, particularly in the villages, they have not changed much, either. They still are an easygoing, basically happy, basically balanced people; beset by a fantastically leaping population, pushing forty million now as against five million in the days of the Ancients, which threatens to burst the fragile economy of the valley of the Nile; worried about problems of war and peace; many of them gravely poor, barely scraping out an existence. Yet they smile, they joke, they release their tensions in noisy, blustering, swiftly ended shouting matches over a bumped fender or a disputed price in the marketplace — and then they smile again.

The goddess Ma'at would know them now. No doubt she does, for she and the other gods and goddesses are still not far away. Photographing at Abu Simbel in the hush of 5:30 A.M., alone with the great temple of Ramesses II and the weird bleak landscape of Nubia and the middle Nile, we saw a white bird flying, heard a single thoughtful cry: god Thoth, god of scribes, wisdom and the arts, in his form of the ibis, was passing by. Sitting on the hotel balcony in Aswan, looking out over the lush green intimacy of Kitchener's Island, we glanced up startled as a hawk swung low, came straight toward us, pulled himself up short, as startled as we, and swung away: god Horus, father and patron of the pharaohs, had shown himself to us. In Luxor, just at twilight one evening, walking along the promenade above the riverbank, there was a blurred impression of movement, a sudden fleeting shadow racing past, fifteen feet below near the water's edge. It paused as if confused, turned, raced back and out of sight — a slim little body, a long bushy tail, two sharp, unmistakable, upstanding ears, a long, narrow, pointed snout: god Anubis, bound on some worried business of his own.

Ten feet high, the ibis stands protectively beside Pharaoh on the temple walls, one hand resting on his shoulder; on the other shoulder, equally protective, rests the hand of the ten-foot falcon. Ten feet high at the entry to the innermost sanctum of Pharaoh's tomb stands the jackal, prepared to guide him into the after-world.

The gods, and the animals that represented them, were sacred. And now Thoth flies wandering and alone with his wistful cry over the desolate reaches of the river at Abu Simbel. And Horus, confused, almost crashes into a balcony of the Oberoi Hotel at Aswan. And Anubis flees for his life along the riverbank at Luxor...

Who were they, these little brown people, averaging perhaps five feet in height, living three, four, five thousand years ago beside a great swift river in the blazing sun, who built so enormously, who made gods of the ibis, the hawk, the jackal and the rest — and made greatest of all the merciless sun that harried them, instead of the swift-flowing river which gave, and still gives, their world its being and its life? Where the transition between the white bird flying, the startled hawk, the furtive jackal, the relentless sun, and the great gods and goddesses who stride with Pharaoh the giant tombs and temples of a fabled land? And whence the serenity that seems to abide with them all — the inner certainty that still, to some degree, and despite all the hectic worries of the modern world, seems to live, at least in some small part, in their almost unbelievably distant descendants?

There are explanations. There is a "science," a "discipline," an "-ology" — Egyptology. Many brilliant scholars, many fine and dedicated men and women, have given, and still give, their lives to it: the patient piecing together, out of a scrap here, a hieroglyph there, a laboriously translated papyrus, some newly discovered tomb, some newly perceived insight into something already discovered, the story of what might have happened during the three millennia of Ancient Egypt's occasionally shaky but generally consistent existence. In some very few areas and some very few eras the knowledge is definite, solid, secure—but most names and most dates are uncertain and open to argument. Egyptologists fall back heavily on phrases such as "in all probability... it seems likely... it seems safe to assume... almost certainly... undoubtedly..."

But there *is* doubt—much doubt—about almost everything; and little *is* certain; and while it seems safe to assume because everybody does assume—*has* to assume, because frequently there is nothing much to go on but assumption—great gaps and holes and areas of pure speculation remain.

It was, after all, a very long time ago; and in the days when the Nile was allowed to be the Nile—before the late Gamal Abdel Nasser came along with his High Dam at Aswan which now gives present-day Egyptians so much worry and so many troubled second thoughts—Lower Egypt was covered over with silt every year. Many, many tombs and temples are undoubtedly—undoubtedly!—lost now beneath the rich farmlands of the Delta and the chaotic streets of Cairo. The great bulk of what we know comes from Upper Egypt, where the annual inundation left silt but only enough to preserve, not bury forever; and where vast areas of desert and sparsely settled land remain, hopeful ground for the expeditions from many countries that patiently dig today, and will continue to dig as long as the world is fascinated by Ancient Egypt; which, it seems safe to say, will be as long as the world is still around to be fascinated by anything.

Out of all the guesses, the assumptions, the poring-over of bits and pieces and the erection thereon of vast new temples of hunch and theory, there has come some reasonably logical concept of what happened in this long, narrow escarpment-protected valley, shorter in length, and much narrower, than the State of California, which housed perhaps the most unique—and for many the most intriguing—of all mankind's civilizations.

In this, geography played a major part, if perhaps not quite the part it has been assigned by more classical Egyptologists. It is true the deserts and "mountain" escarpments—rambling, at times disconnected, rarely rising more than fifteen hundred feet—do provide some natural shelter for the valley and its riverine society; but unless the pharaohs maintained garrisons every mile or so along the ridges, for which there is no evidence, the barrier could have been easily breached at many points by a determined invader. At times it was, most notably in the so-called Hyksos Period, when nomadic peoples of mysterious origin, coming from farther north and east, toppled the pharaonic government and established themselves for the better part of two hundred years as rulers of Egypt; and toward the end when, twilight falling fast, invaders came down the river from Nubia; when Alexander the Great came, died, and left the Ptolemies behind; and finally when the Caesars came, and Ancient Egypt as an independent nation was at last wiped out.

their long story, neither the red crown nor the principal deities of Lower Egypt were lost: they were simply absorbed into the whole.

Menes became the first "Lord of the Two Lands, King of the North and South, Son of the Sun"; the two crowns were combined into the Double Crown. Successive pharaohs at will wore red or white or both, depending on where they happened to be at the time, and moved their capitals up and down the river as it suited them. And Lower Egypt's sun-god Ra, whose original temple site is lost in unknowable antiquity but certainly lies now beneath the broad luxurious streets of Cairo's wealthiest suburb, Heliopolis, was absorbed with his fellows into Upper Egypt's pantheon. The day would come, a thousand years later, when Ra would be joined with Upper Egypt's principal god Amon to form the mightiest deity of them all, Amon-Ra.

There was something very casual, very democratic, very easygoing about all this; something very typical of Ancient Egypt; the beginning, perhaps, of the smile.

At any rate, Menes won and thereafter the Two Lands were one united kingdom, although forever after the distinction between them was maintained, as it is today; and with good reason. Upper and Lower Egypt are noticeably different, particularly in this age of the automobile. The rare flock of cattle or sheep, an occasional horse-drawn carriage, still thread the hooting streets of Cairo; but cattle and sheep are everywhere in Upper Egypt, and the principal sounds of the water-fronts of Luxor and Aswan are the clop-clop of the horse and the agonized Oh-Allah-whatever-am-I-doing-in-this-situation braying of the donkey. The Lower Egyptians are Egyptian, children of many different strains since Menes' day; many Upper Egyptians are Nubians, as they will tell you promptly and proudly. The pace is slower in Upper Egypt, the people equally charming and shrewd but in some ways gentler, more amiable, certainly much more relaxed than their countrymen in the Delta. It is two lands still.

With Menes began what is known to historians as the Early Dynastic Period, running roughly from the time of his conquest, circa 3100 B.C., to about 2686 B.C., the span of the first two dynasties. Then came King Zoser, the Third Dynasty, and the era known as the Old Kingdom, approximately 2686—2181 B.C., a five-hundred-year period of consolidation, the growth of a unified national viewpoint, the development of a national way of doing things.

Zoser proclaimed himself the first god-king of the Two Lands, directed his architect, Imhotep, to build history's first major stone structure, the Step Pyramid at Sakkara, and presided over a time of vigorous expansion and solid growth. Menes' capital of Memphis in the Delta was strengthened and its supremacy further consolidated. Larger boats were constructed for trade up the river and out into the Great Green north along the Phoenician coast to Lebanon. Copper mines in the Sinai were developed; slaves were brought up from Nubia to lead an apparently not very hard life serving court and nobility.

Upper Egypt slumbered, aside from a modest trade with the Memphite court.

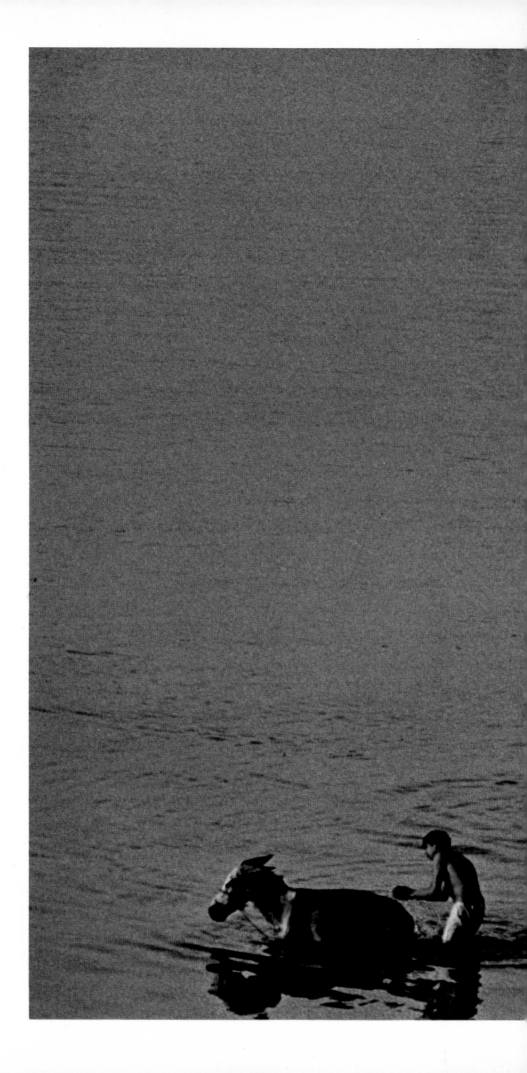

"Whether the visitor walks its bleak banks in far-off Nubia or looks down upon its swift-flowing waters, crowded bridges and roaring corniche traffic from a hotel balcony in Cairo, the Nile is always there, a presence sometimes insistent, sometimes subtle, constant in the mind and being. It is the ka of Egypt, that elusive other-soul of the Ancients, as alive for native and tourist now as it was for them."

With the passing of the Third Dynasty and the inauguration of the Fourth, Egypt acquired the monuments that throughout history have symbolized her in the world's mind more than any others: the construction at Giza—now a suburb half an hour out from downtown Cairo—of the Great Pyramid of Cheops, the slightly smaller pyramid and Sphinx of his son Chephren, and the smaller pyramid of their successor Mycerinas.

Some eighty others, in various conditions of decay, still dot lower Egypt. In front of the three at Giza, Chephren's enigmatic face adorns the Sphinx, rescued from the sands and oblivion first by his very remote successor Tuthmose IV of the Eighteenth Dynasty, and then by Napoleon. He too has survived, but he isn't talking. He, like the Pyramids and all the rest of it, is part of what can only be described as the fun of Ancient Egypt, once you have begun to let your mind and imagination roam over it.

With the Fifth Dynasty came new achievements, including the development of the characteristic forms and conventions which ever after, save for Akhenaten's brief period of "living in truth" reality, were to govern pharaonic art. Commerce and trade expanded to reach as far as Punt, a region probably somewhere in lower Ethiopia or Somalia and always a particular fascination for pharaohs, many of whom mounted expeditions there, the most famous being sweet Hatshepsut's, that tough lady.

Built for somber King Zoser of the Third Dynasty, 2,600 years before Christ, the Step Pyramid broods over the ancient burial ground of Sakkara near Cairo.

In the Sixth Dynasty, however, the grand structure began to fall apart. Pharaoh's government became too big. His personal power became diffused, some of his authority inevitably had to be passed to officials in the field; inevitably some of them began to entertain ambitions and ideas. Pharaoh was first challenged, then subverted, then ignored. What historians know as the First Intermediate Period began. For approximately 150 years all was chaos and confusion in Egypt as rival claimants battled and the peasantry lay low, working hard as always to garner the bounty of Hapi, staying as much as possible out of the way of the armed bands and petty princelings who fought one another up and down the river in inconclusive contests for power.

Ancient Egypt was in her first period of decline; and in the first of her death-defying acts over three thousand years, she came out of it in the traditional way: somebody proved to be tougher, stronger and more tenacious than the rest. Before his victory, however, the feeble and shadowy Seventh, Eighth, Ninth and Tenth Dynasties came and went, their pharaohs virtually unknown and apparently powerless. In Memphis and Heracleopolis, south of the oasis of Fayum, rival kinglets battled for power in the north; and in the south a family of local governors, or "nomarchs," bearing the names In-tef and Men-tu-ho-tep, began to acquire increasing strength—enough so that after some 150 years of universal disorder as the Memphites and Heracleopolitans trailed away, they were able to move north and re-establish effective rule over all of Egypt.

"Lord of the Two Lands, King of the North and South, Son of the Son," once

again became titles not to be taken lightly or scoffed at. The so-called Middle Kingdom, running from about the middle of the Eleventh Dynasty to the end of the Twelfth, c. 2050—1786 B.C., was inaugurated. The reconqueror of the Two Lands was named Mentuhotep II, and his family came from Thebes. The great days of the sleepy village were about to begin; and even though the capital was transferred by various pharaohs to Memphis or other cities, it always came back in time to Thebes, which became and remained the principal city of the Two Lands, thanks in part to a factor ultimately fatal to both the Theban supremacy and to the kingdom.

With the family of Thebes came the god of Thebes. Amon became the supreme national deity, and around him there grew a priesthood that eventually became overweening, enormously powerful and virtually unchallengeable.

All this, however, was far ahead. For the time being all went well with the reunited country. Mentuhotep II vigorously restored order, commerce and trade resumed, the private citizen was safe again in his house and upon the river and the roadways. Soon thereafter the last of Mentuhotep's family, Mentuhotep V, died and A-me-nem-het I, prince of another Theban family, started the Twelfth Dynasty. Building, literature, the arts, trade, commerce, flourished. The Twelfth Dynasty, leaving Thebes, which rapidly became the religious capital as Amon's priesthood grew, established its political capital in the Fayum. For about 250 years its pharaohs ruled over a revived, prosperous and by now increasingly influential Egypt. The inhabitants of the Nile Valley were beginning to look outward. The city-kingdoms scattered along the eastern rim of the Great Green began to feel the impact of Egyptian trade, and, where Pharaoh and his advisers deemed it necessary, Egyptian arms.

Pharaoh had already felt it necessary to organize arms against some of his own unruly subjects. Other nomarchs were still ambitious: it was necessary to form a household army. Amenemhet I named his new capital in the Fayum "Captor of the Two Lands," and he and his successors made sure that this remained the fact.

Abroad, the family of the Twelfth Dynasty made Egypt a fact to be reckoned with also. Amenemhet I and his son Sesostris I pushed vigorously south past the First Cataract, then beyond the Second, and ultimately took much of Nubia. The Libyans, beginning now for the first time to be the chronic problem for Egypt that they still are today, were met and driven back. Advances and consolidations took place northward into the Sinai. Equally vigorous descendants, including several more Amenemhets and Sesostrises, carried on the work. Sesostris III, most able of these, mounted the first expedition against Syria led personally by a pharaoh. At his death Egyptian rule was firm and apparently unchallengeable over a thousand miles of Nile and well up along the eastern rim of the Mediterranean. His son, Amenemhet III, greatly expanded the internal irrigation system, affirmed the laws, promoted trade and stability. "He makes the Two Lands verdant more than a great Nile," his scribes dutifully recorded of him. "He has filled the Two Lands with strength, he is life, cooling the nostrils." Much building of public temples and monuments went on

"Great red-faced Sesostris III, grinning like a prizefighter from the upper gallery of the Luxor Museum..."

under the enlightened family of the Middle Kingdom. Nearly all were destroyed by the ruthless plunderings of the Eighteenth and Nineteenth Dynasties in their endless search for building materials for their own monuments.

Then, once again, came decay. Amenemhet III's son, Amenemhet IV, apparently weak and ineffectual, held things uneasily together for a brief reign of nine years and, having no son, was succeeded by his daughter, the Queen Sebek-nefru-Ra. Four years later she disappeared from history, leaving to the Thirteenth Dynasty a country still outwardly prosperous but awaiting only chance and opportunity for internal tensions to explode again. In a short while they did, and with them, this time, came foreign invasion and kings that knew not Egypt.

Four short reigns of Thirteenth Dynasty kings, and once more nobles and nomarchs were at each other's throats, a wobbly throne again the prize. The "Second Intermediate Period" had begun. From it, the Two Lands again fallen into a scatter of squabbling petty principalities and disunited villages, emerged the Hyksos.

No one today is quite sure who the Hyksos were, but the generally accepted theory is that they were of Arabic and/or Semitic origin, coming from somewhere toward Asia—"shepherd kings," according to the historian Josephus, quoting Manetho, an Egyptian priest who devised, around 300 B.C., out of hearsay, legend and a few scraps of knowledge, the list of dynasties which, for convenience's sake, still governs Ancient Egyptian history today.

Whoever and whatever the Hyksos were, their effect upon Egypt was partial and in no way conducive to the re-establishment of unified government. Their capital was at a place called Avaris, long since lost, in the Delta, leading to the presumption that their main empire and interests must have lain farther east and north in the Euphrates Valley and beyond. Although their very sparse records indicate that some of them claimed control of Upper Egypt, there apparently was no substantial or consistent sovereignty there. Strong families in the south still continued to contend for Thebes and Nubia. In due course, after another interval of chaos and uncertainty lasting for about two hundred years—thus does one capsulize Ancient Egyptian history, two hundred years means almost nothing against three thousand—one of them became strong enough to field an heir with the brains, ability and determination to rid the Two Lands of their foreign invaders. His name was Ah-mo-se I, and with him began the period of Ancient Egypt's greatest power and glory, known as the "the new Kingdom" or "the Empire," c. 1567—1085 B.C.

So began the line of remarkable pharaohs known as the Eighteenth Dynasty, and after them the two remarkable pharaohs of the Nineteenth, Seti I and Ramesses II, followed by Ramesses III of the Twentieth. After them things began to trail away again. But for approximately four hundred years the Two Lands were under the control of strong and dominant personalities who left an unerasable impact upon Egyptian and world history which in some respects has lasted to the present day.

The first Theban ruler to rebel against the Hyksos was Se-ke-nen-Ra; after him came two more of the same name, the second of whom, his skull horribly wounded by the enemy, lies mummified in the Cairo Museum today. Their opposition for a time was stubborn but ineffective, as was that of a King Ke-mo-se who followed them. Then things picked up. Sekenenra III apparently successfully attacked Avaris and began the Hyksos retreat from the Delta; Kemose pushed them farther, with skirmishes into Syria and Palestine; Ahmose conducted the final and definitive campaign that drove them once and for all out of the Delta and out of Egyptian history. There began for Egypt once again a period of stability and order, interrupted only by the short-lived revolution of "the Heretic," "the Criminal," Akhenaten. In time the long-range effects of his rebellion against the priests of Amon would be a major factor in Egypt's final decline; but for four centuries all appeared to go, for the most part, very well. Behind them the Hyksos left two invaluable aids to the creation of empire: the horse and a tradition of organized warfare.

Up to that time, the essentially unwarlike Egyptians had fielded only modest "armies" consisting of few men, poorly equipped and organized, proceeding on foot. Their "wars" and "conquests" were largely carried out by rag, tag, and bobtail troops aided by luck and the equal disorganization of their enemies. With the horse came the concepts of cavalry, militia, organized ground support, strategy. The Egyptians, particularly of the House of Thebes, observed, learned and remembered.

Almost from the moment of assuming the throne the Theban pharaohs found themselves undisputed kings of the Two Lands. Ahmose bequeathed to his son Amon-ho-tep I a complete and unchallenged dominion from Nubia to the Delta. Pharaoh once again was supreme over all.

The form of the newly re-established nation was dictated at first by warfare: the unwarlike became warlike, the peaceful avaricious. Years of battle against the Hyksos had given Ahmose a well-organized and experienced military machine. Its members had fought in Asia and Syria, brought home wealth, plunder and new horizons. Ahmose based his rule on the army. His successors and their officials dreamed of restoring and expanding Egyptian hegemony in the Near East. The priests of Amon, now officially Amon-Ra, dreamed of wealth and power, and got it.

For a long time military state and church state got along very well together. In the fields, as today, the children of Hapi moved to the flow of the river, planted their crops, garnered their harvests, kept to their peaceful ways; except, as today, when called to Pharaoh's cause and the maw of foreign wars. Government settled into the form that was already, for the Eighteenth Dynasty, a thousand years ago and ancient history: the pyramidal. The Son of the Sun was at the top, all else falling neatly away below him.

Pharaonic government became intimate and personalized at the same time as it became remote and ceremonial. Pharaoh began the day with the worship of Amon, and with his worship the day began officially for his people. He took a direct hand in the affairs of government; his word was absolute and he exercised its power absolutely. But aside from his family and his highest circle of officials, headed by viziers for North and South, he was on a plane no ordinary mortal could come near. And increasingly Amon was at his elbow. Amon gave approval and benediction to his works, Amon presided over his battles, his glories and his triumphs. Amon was rewarded accordingly.

Until Amonhotep IV; and then, briefly, Amon's vast structure fell apart. But it, like Egypt, was put back together again for another thousand years; and to this day in the temples one can occasionally see a white-coated figure bowing, with some cabalistic sign, to the figure of the god. Not many do this, and who knows what it means to them? But a few do; and every day with their presence the tourists worship by the thousands in Amon's temple; and who can say with entire truth that Amon is not living still?

So the Eighteenth Dynasty grew and flourished. Amonhotep I again consolidated Egypt's control of Nubia to the second cataract, though the area south from there to the fourth cataract, known as Kush—and because of its presumptuous rebelliousness, always as "wretched Kush" or "vile Kush" in the official records—was never quite subdued in his lifetime. The Libyans, by now a chronic headache, were once more driven back. Forays, inconclusive but far-ranging, struck into Syria and the Euphrates Valley. Egypt was at last on the warpath and the wars were real: severed enemy hands were the surest proofs with which to gain favor from the king.

Amonhotep I died at Thebes. A successor, Tuthmose I, son of a nonroyal mother, was crowned pharaoh, having consolidated his claim to the throne by prudently marrying a royal princess, Ahmose, of the old royal line that had expelled the Hyksos. Nubia still demanded attention.

Tuthmose reached the third cataract, beat the Nubians, returned to Thebes with the body of a Nubian chieftain hanging head downward from the prow of the royal barge. He then turned north, to proceed successfully as far as Naharin, which means "land of the rivers," the region between the Euphrates and the Orontes, and set a boundary stela in Syria to demark the northernmost limits of the empire. Tribute from the jumble of Middle Eastern city-states along the Mediterranean flowed into the treasury and from there to Amon, whose priests blessed all that Pharaoh did. Tuthmose returned to Thebes to preside for most of his remaining years over an expanded, prosperous and unchallenged state. He was succeeded by two remarkable children who fought one another bitterly for the throne for twenty years until the male, Tuthmose III, finally defeated his half sister, Hatshepsut, and assumed sole rule.

During her periods of dominance in their seesaw battle, Hatshepsut virtually banished Tuthmose III to Nubia; built her beautiful funerary temple at Deir el-Bahri, in a cove of the hills directly across from Luxor; organized her famous expedition to Punt; raised obelisks at the already-cluttered Temple of Amon at Karnak; and directed the construction of many other temples and monuments to the glory of the god along the Nile. Being a woman, she led no expeditions of war nor was she faced with the need for any, as all was calm on Egypt's borders and the tribute rolled faithfully in. Tuthmose III was made of sterner stuff. His incessant schemes to secure

"You are verdant, O Nile, you are verdant, you that makes man to live on his cattle and his cattle on the meadow. You are verdant, you are verdant; O Nile, you are verdant.

Tuthmose III vowed that he would "overthrow that vile enemy and extend the boundaries of Egypt in accordance with the command of my father, Amon-Ra." And so he did, smiting his foes with a joyous gusto.

support from the Amon priesthood and the nobility for his restoration finally succeeded; and Hatshepsut, too, vanished.

Once he had disposed of her, most likely by some form of poison or starvation, he first saw to it that all her monuments were desecrated, that her face, figure, name and titularies were chiseled out and that the details of her reign were obliterated as much as possible — a job half-heartedly done, apparently, by those ordered to do it, for Deir el-Bahri still contains records of the expedition to Punt, her claimed holy birth, and other details of her reign; and statues of her smiling, self-confident, obviously determined little person still abound in the Cairo Museum, the Metropolitan Museum in New York, and elsewhere. But enough was done to make the pharaonic point: Tuthmose III was in charge, the immediate past did not exist because he commanded that it not exist; and he was now free to embark upon the great scheme of conquest which was to make him the most aggressive and successful of all the warrior pharaohs. Once he had removed his difficult relation from his path, he marched into Asia to attack a coalition of Middle Eastern ministates led by the king of Kadesh. Northern Palestine, Syria, Naharin and the newly risen power of Mittani, east of the Euphrates, were all ranged against him. He raised an army of perhaps twenty thousand men, trained it rigorously and set forth, as he put it, "to overthrow that vile enemy and extend the boundaries of Egypt in accordance with the command of my father, Amon-Ra."

Presently he came to the fortress of Megiddo, overlooking the plain of Jezreel from the north slope of the Carmel range. It was the key to his enemies' defense. A lengthy siege was necessary to reduce it, but Tuthmose summed up succinctly the reason why: "All the princes of all the northern countries are cooped up within it. The capture of Megiddo is the capture of a thousand towns."

It was not, however, the subjugation of all the petty states that had rallied against him; between year 23 and year 39 of his reign, fourteen separate campaigns were necessary before the northeast was finally reduced. An Egyptian peace at last fell on the area; and powerful kingdoms on its outer edges, including Assyria, Babylon and the Hittites, prudently began sending gifts and declarations of friendship to Pharaoh. Annual tribute also came in regularly from the defeated city-states. Significantly, on his return from the capture of Megiddo, he gave to Amon in gratitude three towns he had captured in southern Lebanon, together with much captured gold, silver and many jewels. He also gave the god extensive lands in both Upper and Lower Egypt, herds of cattle and sheep, and a sizable number of his Asiatic prisoners to serve as slaves in the temples.

Suddenly Amon's fortune, like Amon's official status, was greater than that of all the other gods combined. Quite inadvertently, Tuthmose had set the priesthood on the collision course with the crown which was ultimately to bring about the "revolution" of his great-great-grandson Akhenaten, with all its attendant consequences for god, crown and the Two Lands.

Tuthmose brought the Egyptian empire to its zenith. At his death, it all collapsed

Immediately the north was in revolt again; and now it was the task of his son, Amonhotep II, to subjugate it once more. Being the very able son of a very able father, he proceeded to do so with briskness and dispatch. In his second year as Pharaoh he launched a blitz that took him, between early April and mid-June, all the way from the Delta to the kingdom of Mittani, conquering and restoring as he went. Everything fell before him, and even proud Mittani, unconquered by his father, sent its leaders to beg for mercy — "a mighty occurrence, it has never been heard since the time of the gods. This country, which knew not Egypt, beseeches the Good God." The Good God accepted the supplication, and when he returned to Memphis, did so with many prisoners and an eye for theater. He wanted no more revolts, and he got none. He arranged a lesson that was not forgotten for some time.

He brought with him as prisoners more than 500 chieftains of northern Syria, 240 of their women, 210 horses and 300 chariots. When he proceeded upriver to Thebes he arrived with the seven "kings" of a city-state known as Tikhsi hanging head downward from the prow of his barge. Ashore, he ordered them taken at once to Karnak and there sacrificed them himself in the presence of the statue of Amon. Six of their bodies he ordered hung from the walls; the seventh he ordered taken immediately to Nubia, which was being difficult again. He was determined to put a stop to that, too. The unfortunate kinglet's body was hung from the walls at Napata in the region of Karoy, just below the fourth cataract. The point was made, the expedition was successful, and the restless Nubians settled down. For several centuries thereafter Napata, well-garrisoned and maintained, was officially the southern outpost of Egypt.

Amonhotep II ruled for approximately twenty-four years more in peace after these emphatic demonstrations of his will. He was a man of powerful build who claimed that none but himself could draw his crossbow. Still preserved, it bears his name and the proud boast: "Smiter of the Troglodytes, overthrower of Kush, hacking up their cities... the great Wall of Egypt, protecting his soldiers." Great Wall he seems to have been. Behind it the Two Lands and their by now far-flung dominions enjoyed a quarter of a century of stability.

With the accession of Tuthmose IV, however, the pattern of rebellion was once again repeated; and showing decisiveness worthy of his father and grandfather, he also put a prompt stop to it with an expedition as far north as Mittani, subduing as he went. With Mittani he finally arranged the strong and relatively permanent alliance both kingdoms had been seeking for some years, receiving among other things Mutemwaya, the daughter of the king, to be his queen. The second of the Eighteenth Dynasty's strong ladies, she became the mother of Amonhotep III, who presided over the gradual decline of the golden age and, by fathering Akhenaten, brought to an unexpected and drastic end the first phase of empire.

All pharaohs loved to have themselves portrayed as roundly chastising their enemies. When you had entire temple walls on which to tell your story, there was no end to it.

For a time, however, Amonhotep III and his own strong-willed Queen Tiye, whose resin-blackened bust in the Cairo Museum has prompted some thought, otherwise unfounded, that she might have been Nubian, ruled together in peace and splendor. Amonhotep obviously loved her dearly, for he promptly inserted her name immediately after his in all royal proclamations and gave her a prominence and an active role in government which made her virtually co-ruler of the Two Lands. Counter to their actions with his three immediate predecessors, the Asiatics did not revolt at his accession; four years after he came to the crown, the Nubians did, and he had to go south to subdue them. It was his first and last military venture. From then on Nubia to the fourth cataract was undisputedly Egyptian, and as far as the second was almost entirely Egyptianized, with the building of many temples, the worship of Amon and the other gods, and a steady trade.

So Amonhotep and Tiye presided with serene confidence over their empire, enjoying peaceful relations with all its many kinglets and the larger states, such as Babylon, Mittani, Assyria and even Cyprus, on its perimeters. Amonhotep, though a steady builder who ordered the Temple of Luxor to be built, added to and embellished Karnak, and built many temples to himself and the gods up and down the Nile, was also the most self-indulgent of all the pharaohs. It seemed to him and to Tiye a truly golden age; except that in their own household a strange son was growing who was destined to bring upon the crown and upon the Two Lands a disaster from which neither was ever fully to recover.

At first Amonhotep IV appears to have been a normal child; but at some point in early youth the grotesque malformations, before which the visitor to his statues in the Cairo Museum stands in troubled wonderment, began to creep upon him. His disease, a glandular disturbance of some sort, has not been absolutely diagnosed across the gulf of 3,300 years; some guesses are more logical than others, and some writers bolder than others in asserting the true nature of his ailment. In any event, it occurred; and because of it he was set upon a lonely path that was to lead to the complete disruption of Egyptian society, the loss of the empire, and a challenge to the gods and to the power and inviolability of the crown which came very near to destroying the country altogether.

Soon after he was made co-regent with his father at the age of fifteen, he began to pay more and more open tribute to the Aten—the sun disk itself, as opposed to the sun at its various stages of rising and setting which together had become amalgamated over the centuries into the concept of Ra and had then been absorbed into Amon-Ra and the great priesthood. By now the priests of Amon were almost co-equal with Pharaoh; he could do nothing without Amon's blessing and support, and he could do nothing to defy Amon's power. Or so, at least, thought every pharaoh down to Amonhotep III. Amonhotep IV took it one step further. Prompted by his illness, inspired by a determined fanaticism and what can only be respected—when one visits the massive ruins of Karnak and reflects on the enormous power of Amon—as a very great personal courage indeed, he set forth to reverse the course of millennia. Amon and the other gods were banished, their priesthoods dispersed, their temples closed, their wealth and power summarily transferred to the Aten.

For the first time in known history, the concept of a single God was officially proclaimed: in the Nile Valley, by an extremely odd, unique and mysterious human being who happened to be a god himself.

In due time, of course, the effort failed. His health, never robust, declined. His people, steeped for so many, many centuries in the worship of the gods and of Amon, did not respond. His family conspired. By then the empire was gone: he never acknowledged the pleading letters that came from the north desperately requesting his help against growing threats of subversion and conquest, and all soon fell away. The society was in complete disarray, the Two Lands were lost in uncertainty and confusion. He died, perhaps naturally, more likely in violence and despair; was succeeded by his youngest brother, Tutankhamon, who was supported by their uncle Aye and their ambitious and tough-minded cousin, Horemheb; and the Amarna story ended. Its consequences would have much to do with the ultimate fall of Ancient Egypt.

For the time being, and for perhaps a century and a half thereafter, however, the restoration of Amon under Tutankhamon—who was forced to change his name from "Tutankhaten," originally a tribute to his brother's god—appeared to end the country's troubles and return it to the official certainty and serenity to which it had clung, through good centuries and bad, for almost two thousand years. But it was not until Tutankhamon, still faithful to the Aten tradition, had been ruthlessly disposed of at age eighteen after a reign of nine years, and the aged Aye had followed him for four more feeble years, that tireless and persistent Horemheb took over and began the full restoration of Amon.

His reign of thirty years or a little more was the reign of the military man he was: iron-handed, dictatorial, uncompromising, but just, as he saw the greatest need of Egypt, which in his mind and those of a great majority of his countrymen, was to be speedily restored to the condition of peace, stability and *ma'at* which Akhenaten had so violently wrenched out of shape.

When Horemheb died in his seventies, his equally aged successor was his longtime friend and comrade-in-arms, the general who took the name Ramesses I and founded the Nineteenth Dynasty. He lived a year, left the throne to his vigorous and determined son, Seti I. Seti and his son, Ramesses II, whom we left sitting patiently in the dark at Abu Simbel awaiting the return of Ra, were the last of the great pharaohs who dreamed, and made the dream come at least partially true, of restoring the lost power and glory of the two Lands. After them the story is one of long and irreversible decline that lingered on for another thousand years but produced few pharaohs of any real significance until the last Cleopatra of the Ptolemies, whose gift to Egypt was that she lost it.

Seti reconquered perhaps a third of the territory his predecessors prior to

He is the only pharaoh who lies in his original tomb in the Valley of the Kings at Luxor: the murdered boy of nineteen whose brief and undistinguished reign, 3,300 years ago, revived in lasting glory when his tomb was discovered in A.D. 1922 and his fame went forth to the ends of the earth as Tutankhamon.

Akhenaten had held, but it soon became apparent that the aggressiveness of the Hittites would require either constant warfare or a treaty of peace. His people were no longer geared to war and conquest as they had been under great warrior kings. Sadly but practically, Seti signed a treaty of peace with the Hittites and turned to the repair of the temples and monuments, only partially restored by Horemheb, which had been destroyed by Akhenaten. Amon returned to his fullest glory.

Once again the King of the Gods reigned supreme over all the other gods and over the land. During Seti's time and that of his son, the priesthood rose to its greatest wealth, possessing more than 691,334 acres of land, 65 cities and towns, 421,000 head of cattle, 81,000 slaves, 433 orchards and gardens, 83 ships, 53 building yards and more than 5,000 statues to attest to Amon's divinity.

Seti's reign lasted perhaps two decades, his two major legacies, aside from extensive additions to the Temple of Karnak, being perhaps the loveliest of all Egyptian temples, at Abydos, and his own tomb, today the most extensive and most colorful of all those preserved in the Valley of the Kings.

After him came Ramesses II, who found on his accession that the north was once more in revolt, the Hittites were once more threatening and he must begin anew the heavy task of trying to reconquer what Egypt had held before Akhenaten let it slip away. This he succeeded in doing with partial success in the first fifteen years of his reign; and apparently would have continued to slog away at it, had not the king of the Hittites, Metella, suddenly died and left his kingdom in the hands of his much weaker brother, Khetasar. Khetasar had his own problems at home, and as a result of them suddenly sent Ramesses a proposal for a treaty of alliance and permanent peace. With hastily concealed surprise and suitable dignity, Ramesses accepted. The treaty held, and thirteen years later Khetasar actually visited the Theban court, his purpose being to bring his daughter for marriage to Pharaoh.

So Ramesses married (for perhaps the sixtieth time, at that point) and went no more to war. Only two of his successors ever warred again with any real determination. Sporadic attempts were made from time to time down the centuries, usually with hired mercenaries, to recapture bits of Syria and Palestine, but aside from those of Mer-nep-tah and Ramesses III, none ever really succeeded. Unnoticed but inexorable, the long twilight had begun.

Ramesses was succeeded by his thirteenth son, Merneptah, himself an old man by the time his father died. Revolts occurred in the north, on the west the Libyans were again active. A series of holding actions that were to last the better part of six hundred years began. When Merneptah's forces won the first one and defeated the Libyans, the Egyptians, as reported by Breasted, and described by Merneptah's scribes at Merneptah's orders, rejoiced:

"Great joy has come in Egypt, rejoicing comes forth from the towns of Egypt. They talk of the victories which Merneptah has achieved among the Libyans: 'How amiable is he, the victorious ruler! How magnified is the king among the gods! How fortunate is he, the commanding Lord! Sit happily down and talk, or walk far out

Ramesses II left effigies of himself everywhere but none is more impressive than this striking likeness in the ancient capital of Memphis.

44

upon the way, for there is no fear in the heart of the people.' The strongholds are left to themselves, the wells are opened again. The messengers skirt the battlements of the walls, shaded from the sun, until their watchmen wake. The soldiers lie sleeping and the border scouts are in the field of their own free will. The herds of the field are left as cattle sent forth without herdsman, crossing at will the fullness of the stream. There is no uplifting of a shout in the night: 'Stop! Behold one comes, one comes with the speech of strangers! One comes and goes with singing, and there is no lamentation of mourning people.' The towns are settled again anew; and as for one that ploweth his harvest, he shall eat of it. Ra has returned himself to Egypt; he was born destined to be her protector, even the king Merneptah.'"

Never again would there be quite that note of joyous relief in Egypt. From now on, with brief flashes of light that temporarily pushed back but did not halt the encroaching darkness, it was all downhill.

Merneptah died, dynastic struggles broke out, Nineteenth Dynasty gave way to Twentieth and a long line of minor Ramesses whose lack of distinction was broken only by Ramesses III. He successfully defeated the Libyans once again and also won a sea battle along the Phoenician coast against invaders who were pushing steadily down through Syria and Palestine. The victory reasserted Egyptian sovereignty over a small portion of the vast domains once held in Syria. It did not stop the ceaseless pressures against the borders.

But for a time all seemed tranquil, as in the old days. Tribute, though from a much-reduced hegemony, once more came regularly into Thebes. Trade with Asia and across the Great Green to Cyprus flourished. Domestic safety was assured and the children of Hapi once more tilled their soil in security and peace. The last of the Theban temples, Medinet Habu, on the western plain south of the necropolis, was greatly expanded and embellished by Ramesses III to the glory of Amon and for the recording of his own battles. And in a fashion more fateful than he knew, he also lavished gifts of great wealth upon the major gods, most of all upon Amon, whose priesthood once again virtually ran the country in uneasy association with the palace.

In the Eighteenth Dynasty the High Priest of Amon had become head of all the priesthoods; in the Nineteenth Dynasty the High Priesthood had become hereditary. Amon's temple at Karnak became the repository for not only his own records but those of all other priesthoods as well; insidiously and with great determination his priests steadily increased their control over all the other priesthoods. A kingship, in effect, had developed alongside the kingship; and Pharaoh found himself at last in the position Akhenaten had greatly feared and bitterly fought against, that of being Amon's virtual prisoner. The god to whom Tuthmose III had given the first gift of three towns in Syria had grown at last, through many gifts and much dutiful obedience by monarchs of the Eighteenth, Nineteenth and Twentieth Dynasties, into a monster.

Against this Ramesses III, like his successors, had few weapons with which to

46

fight: a mercenary army whose loyalty could not be relied upon, a personal household largely composed of slaves drawn from foreign battles, equally unreliable; a harem filled with little princes whose ambitious mothers constantly intrigued to set their sons upon the throne. Finally one such attempt reached serious proportions. With the connivance of the priesthood a young pretender was found agreeable to Amon: Pharaoh's life was genuinely threatened. He discovered it, ordered a trial, lived to see thirty-two of the defendants, including his ambitious son and the boy's mother, convicted. He directed that the guilty be permitted to take their own lives and shortly thereafter died, last of the imperial pharaohs and an embittered and solitary man.

From that point on the story is quickly told on paper, though it took another thirteen hundred years to work itself out. Nine more bearers of the proud name of Ramesses, all weaklings, pass in review and, without distinction, into history. By the time of Ramesses XII, about 1090 B.C., the High Priest of Amon, Hrihor, moves triumphantly, as shadowy Ramesses XII disappears, to assume the full titles and titularies of the Pharaoh.

Amon triumphant in Thebes, however, proves not to be Amon triumphant over all, though Hrihor and his priestly successors blandly continue to insist in their official proclamations that they have effective rule over the Two Lands and are still receiving tribute from the empire. Empire, and the Two Lands as a political entity, are both gone; but as always in Ancient Egypt, the fiction, often enough reiterated, is proclaimed to be the fact.

Shadowy dynasties now come and go through the revolving door of history. The Twenty-first trails away, the Twenty-second, composed of Libyan immigrants infiltrating the Delta from the west, takes power under a pharaoh named Sheshonk. Although a vigorous and effective man, he is unable to really reunite the disunited Two Lands, and so he accepts something of the feudal arrangements of pre-dynastic times three thousand years before. Once again, after many empty years, a pharaoh moves north and invades Palestine; once again, a united kingdom enjoys a brief spark of renewed trade, prosperity and stability. But the division of the Two Lands into a set of almost independent principalities, which Sheshonk I is unable to stop, makes the task impossible.

Civil war breaks out, the Twenty-second Dynasty ends, a Twenty-third, also Libyan, assumes power. But the explosive forces are too great. The rule of Pharaoh becomes ever more tenuous, finally collapses. Up from the south come, at last, the Nubians, bearing Nubian names but being careful, as with all Egypt's invaders, to retain the old titles and claim the old power: Pharaoh is still Lord of the Two Lands, King of the North and South, Son of the Sun, though his name now may be Ta-ke-lot or Sha-ba-ka or Ta-har-ka. The Twenty-fourth and Twenty-fifth hurry by, filled with fighting, confusions, distress to the children of Hapi and the Two Lands. The now dominant power of Asia, Asyria, angered by Egypt's lingering pretensions to Palestine, invades and conquers Lower Egypt. The most able of the Nubians,

Taharka, flees to Upper Egypt and takes command of Thebes, where Amon's priesthood is at last declining, split by factionalism and unable to maintain the god's supremacy in a constantly harried and divided land.

The aging Taharka eventually appoints a co-regent, Ta-nut-Amon, who, a year after Taharka's death, once more invades Lower Egypt, wins an ephemeral victory over the Assyrian garrison in Memphis, settles in Memphis and proclaims himself ruler of all Egypt. Ashurbanipal, now king of Assyria, determines to conquer Egypt once and for all, invades, triumphs, captures Thebes, drives Tanutamon south to Napata, from which the Nubians never again emerge to seek control of Egypt. One last bright moment remains before all declines into final emptiness. From Sais in the central Delta emerges the family of the Twenty-sixth Dynasty, and with them a valedictory flare before the final night.

Psam-tik I of Sais seizes the opportunity offered by the war between Ashurbanipal and his brother, king of Babylon, to assert his own supremacy in the Delta, to move from there to the speedy conquest of all of Lower Egypt, from there to Thebes and control of Upper Egypt. Once again in the midst of general chaos, one strong man cuts through and for a brief moment it is as though all the centuries of trouble had never been, as though the Two Lands were reborn in all their ancient glory. Civil rebellion is suppressed, laws restored; the fading fortune of Amon is placed by Psamtik in the hands of his daughter Nitocris, who becomes High-Priestess of Amon; all is at peace within the land. And with a determination both touching and pathetic, Psamtik and his descendants of the Twenty-sixth Dynasty make a desperate national effort, in art, in literature, in music, in dress, in customs, in every phase of society, to imitate in exact detail what seems to them the ideal period in all of their long history — the great days of the Old Kingdom, two thousand years before.

Consciously and deliberately, everything is revived as if all between had been wiped out. The pyramids of the kings who ruled at Memphis so long ago are renovated and restored. Their worship becomes official, their mortuary services are reactivated and re-endowed. The ancient titles come back into use, the customs of that far-off court are revived; even the writing and language is cleansed of its more modern elements, and pharaohs and officials speak and write in the archaic tongue not used for many centuries. Religion is rid of all its foreign intrusions, the old ways of ritual and worship are re-established. Tombs once more are painted with the ancient conventional scenes of fishermen and hunters, shipyard workers, musicians, workers in the vineyards, the cheerful life of everyday. The ancient irrigation system is refurbished and strengthened. It is as though the Saite Dynasty were King Canute saying to the sea, "Go back." And the sea does go back, two thousand years.

But not, of course, for long. A brave, gallant, wistful and hopelessly futile attempt runs aground on the basic fact: this is today, not two thousand years ago. Art begins to drift into a better, more lifelike form; religion, seeking to turn back, only results in a proliferation of new gods and goddesses, with more and more animals becoming sacred as their representatives. Amon does not return. And Psamtik, native of the Delta, observer of the trade maintained by the Assyrians with their Mediterranean neighbors, opens the door and deliberately encourages the inflow of Syrian, Semitic and, most importantly, Greek traders into his country. For the first time the exclusive Egyptians find sizable numbers of foreigners permitted to live in their midst. Greek merchants are followed by an increasing employment of Greek soldiers in the Saite army. And the clock, set to tick at two thousand years ago, inexorably lurches ahead and resumes a current rhythm.

Though he holds himself aloof from this, the average Egyptian cannot help but be affected by his pharaohs' increasingly Hellenistic bent; and as for the Greeks, they are intrigued, bedazzled and overwhelmed by the mysterious civilization in which they find themselves. Trade, artistic forms, monuments, temples—the very fact of Egypt itself—impinge heavily upon the Greek consciousness. The mystique of Ancient Egypt begins, grows, flourishes in the awed minds and through the awed pens of the Greeks: theirs is the principal conduit through which it comes to the Western world for almost two thousand years, until Napoleon's invasion in A.D. 1798, the discovery of the Rosetta Stone and Champollion's translation of the hieroglyphics finally unlocks the sleeping centuries. With fateful consequences for Egypt, the mystique eventually takes root in the mind of a youth from Macedon who will not be satisfied until he has conquered everything, particularly the most mysterious land of all. But that is still three hundred years after Psamtik's time.

First comes Psamtik's son Ne-cho and one more attempt—this time truly the last—to reconquer Asia. In two years Necho surges north—wins a decisive battle at Megiddo where Tuthmose III first established Egyptian power nine hundred years before—appears to have re-established the empire—and before the two years end, is defeated by Nebuchadnezzar of Babylon and driven back. Nebuchadnezzar offers a treaty of peace, Necho accepts. Thereafter, as reported in II Kings 24:7, "...the king of Egypt came not again any more out of his land; for the king of Babylon had taken, from the brook of Egypt (which must be the Old Testament's disparaging put-down of the Nile) unto the river Euphrates, all that pertained to the king of Egypt."

The Twenty-sixth Dynasty trails down through a few more minor kings, one of whom, Amasis, is given the epithet "Philhellene," which fairly well sums up his family's attitude toward the Greeks. After a reign of forty-four convivial years he dies and passes on his throne to his son Psamtik III, who is promptly defeated by the Persians under Cambyses.

Manetho lists eight Persian kings in the Twenty-seventh Dynasty, several of whom, including Artaxerxes I and Darius II, never deign to visit their Egyptian colony, though all are careful as always to include Pharaoh's titularies with their own. Sporadic and half-hearted contests occur from time to time. A Sais king recaptures the throne from the Persians to form Manethos' Twenty-eighth Dynasty, followed by four or five more Egyptians from Mendes. Three more from Sebennytus form the Thirtieth Dynasty, its last Pharaoh, Nec-ta-ne-bos, being the last native Egyptian to hold the throne.

Then three Persians return to make up the Thirty-first Dynasty. The last of these, Darius III, has the misfortune to stand in the way of a world force, the youth from Macedon. Alexander the Great defeats him, moves on to Egypt in 332 B.C., takes it, returns to Babylon to die at age thirty-two—but not before, like all the rest, he has been deified and formally crowned Lord of the Two Lands, King of the North and South, Son of the Sun.

The Macedonian invasion dies with its leader, but behind him he leaves the general Ptolemy, who assumes the throne to found the last dynasty. The Ptolemies survive for approximately 360 years, ending when Cleopatra, fully crowned Pharaoh like her very distant predecessor Hatshepsut, but living in a much tougher world, is unable to keep either her head or her throne in the midst of the fiercely contending generals who seek the crown of Rome. Defeated by Octavian, she and her lover Antony commit suicide; and Egypt passes at last into the hands of the long line of foreign rulers who will continue until independence is finally wrested from the British in A.D. 1949, five thousand years after Menes established the throne of the united Two Lands.

"There shall be no more a prince out of Egypt," prophesied Ezekiel; but history does not always know the word never. Once more a native Egyptian rules Kemet. The title now is President, but he is still, for many practical purposes, Lord of the Two Lands, King of the North and South; and, insofar as individual abilities permit, Son of the Sun.

The manager of the airport at Abu Simbel, that most excellent man, works his miracle, finds space. The plane swings up and away. Lake Nasser and the bleak expanse of Nubia flow swiftly beneath. Ramesses and his mighty temple rapidly disappear. Bare, empty of people, filled with strange humps and hillocks left over from days far beyond the pre-dynastic, the desert keeps one company down to Aswan. The flight is approximately twenty-five minutes, the change in country not noticeable from the air. The hills are still brown and barren, the river stark blue. At first no vegetation is visible at the militarily guarded airport from which one is transported by bus to town. Off to the right one sees the tall white monument to Nasser, the straight line of the High Dam, the end of the lake. Abruptly the Nile becomes a true river again, plunging through shallow canyons, crevasses, secret passageways among the rocks. Trees and abundant greenery suddenly appear. We are at the First Cataract, the ancient boundary of the Old Kingdom from which later pharaohs moved south in their recurring campaigns against "wretched Kush."

More significantly, we are now in the heart of Nubia. Many Nubian villages were uprooted, their inhabitants forcibly moved lock, stock and barrel to make way for Lake Nasser. Not so fortunate as Ramesses, they had no worldwide effort mounted for them. It was left to the Egyptian Government, which, according to its lights and limited funds, did the best it could to resettle its darker-skinned citizens in comfortable surroundings. Houses were built in the Nubian style, some of them very substantial, indistinguishable from the small-domed villages that still exist in isolated areas away from the lake. Schools were established, health services set up. The attempt was made to transfer people in the same fashion as Ramesses was transferred—not *in situ* as he was, but to circumstances as close as possible to those they had left.

The experiment did not altogether succeed despite the government's earnest and sincere efforts. The Nubians, a proud and handsome people with features more aquiline and sharply defined than those of their black cousins farther south in Africa, are still not much reconciled to it. A decade has passed and there is still unhappiness and resentment, though there is no overt attempt to change the situation—and no real power to do so, either. Now, as always, the Nubians are subject to the power of the central government. No one now would depict them so crudely as the pharaohs always did—even mild, unhappy little Tutankhamon is shown with his heel on the neck of a black—but there is a distinction, not always very subtle. The Delta looks down on the people of Upper Egypt—the Delta looks down on everybody—just as the Delta always has. Nowadays many Nubians have gone north to Cairo, but the jobs they get are generally what might be expected: waiters, porters, minor employees in hotels, household servants. Very few Nubians reach prominent positions in the government of today's Two Lands: wretched Kush is wretched still in some ways, though her people's naturally sunny, good-natured, easygoing and charitable dispositon inhibits much outward show of bitterness. The Nubians can always be counted upon to joke, to laugh, to sing, to make the cheerful best of their lot. It gives to Aswan and to Luxor, their two principal places of residence now, an air

The temple of Philae at Aswan, like that of Ramesses II at Abu Simbel, is being relocated to escape the voracious waters of Lake Nasser. Beneath its Greco-Roman ruins on the original site excavators were forced to abandon earlier temples whose roofs go back unknown centuries into the earliest mists of Egypt.

Lord Kitchener was given an island at Aswan in the days when Britain ruled Egypt. Now the island forms a refuge for tourists, souvenir vendors and the white ibis, which in ancient times were known as the embodiment of the god Thoth, deity of scribes and wisdom.

of general, welcoming goodwill that is not always found in Cairo, Alexandria and other cities farther down the river. It is also the principal reason why Upper Egypt has the relaxed air it does, and why the tourist, whether he analyzes it or not, feels instantly at home when he arrives there.

Aswan today is the site of the President's retreat, the villa and mausoleum of the late Agha Khan, the regular winter residence of his widow the Begum, the vacation resort, still, for some British, Europeans and Americans who like its leisurely pace and relative freedom from tourists. Tourists come, but they do not stay long: there are, after all, only four really major items to see. One is the High Dam, a presumed military objective in time of war—not the least of modern Egypt's worries being what would happen to the entire valley and the Delta cities—to say nothing of the Great Green itself—if somebody bombed Gamal Nasser's dream-child and released the horrible force of all that impounded water. The second sight is the Temple of Philae, a creation principally of Ptolemaic and Roman times—though when it was hoisted out of Lake Nasser and removed, like Abu Simbel, to safe higher ground, the roofs of even more ancient temples were found below, which had to be left to perish.

The third is the island given Lord Kitchener during British days, which now forms a lushly wooded, tranquilly idyllic spot for tourists to wander and vendors of ready-made antiquities and bead caps to pester them. And the fourth is the pharaonic quarry from which came the characteristic mottled red-and-gray granite of the royal statues, the statues of the gods, and the obelisks.

An obelisk lies there still for the visitor to walk upon, ordered by some unknown pharaoh of the twilight, never finished, never moved, never even identified by the cartouche of him who commanded it. It looks somehow pathetic, lying there. Like so many of Egypt's relics, it prompts thoughts of mortality—*sic transit gloria*—the emptiness of power—and all the other cliches that normally go with such sights. They seem to mean a little more in Egypt than they do elsewhere, though. There *was* a lot of gloria, and it transited a long, long time ago.

Not so with the original iron butterfly, however. One balmy evening in Thebes sweet Hatshepsut got to thinking:

"I sat in the palace, I remembered him who fashioned me [her God, Amon, since she would not accord Tuthmose I that honor, though he happened to be in her mother's bedchamber at the time of her conception], my heart led me to make for him two obelisks of electrum [a mixture of gold and silver], whose points mingled with heaven." They were 97½ feet high, weighed 350 tons each and were the tallest structures erected in Egypt to that time. "Their rays," she reported complacently, "flood the Two Lands when the sun rises between them as he dawns in the horizon of heaven."

Her lover Sen-mut, father of her daughter Nef-ru-Ra, royal architect, builder and general overseer of all her projects, successfully supervised their creation at Aswan. The work took seven months, and when completed the obelisks were

Modern yet curiously ancient, the tomb of the Aga Khan dominates the west bank of the Nile at Aswan.

56

From the quarry at Aswan came the rose granite the pharaohs used for their temples, statues and obelisks. This never-completed obelisk bears mute witness to the pharaonic urge to self-glorification. No mark remains to show whom it was supposed to honor.

brought downriver end to end on a huge barge towed by 30 galleys employing 960 oarsmen. The lady knew exactly where to put them.

Although she herself had been presented to the court by her father, Tuthmose I, as his successor when she was still a small child, and had strengthened her claim to the throne by later designating Amon as her true parent, bothersome Tuthmose III also had a dramatic claim to make. During his youth he was relegated by his father, as the son of a minor concubine, to the post of lesser priest of Amon at Karnak. With Amon's help he soon took care of that.

One day when Tuthmose I was in his temple at Karnak presenting oblations to the god, his son was standing among the ranks of ordinary priests. Other priests were carrying the statue of Amon around the circumference. Suddenly the god made them halt in front of Tuthmose III. The young prince fell to the ground in worship, but lo and behold, Amon raised him up and, ignoring the aging Tuthmose I, led Tuthmose III to the "Station of the King" where only Pharaoh might stand while rendering tribute. A great shout went up: Tuthmose I looked around in a daze and suddenly found himself pharaoh no longer. His age saved him, he was allowed to live out his short remaining time in peace; and Tuthmose III, brushing aside Hatshepsut's legitimate claims, began to rule alone. Before long, however, nobles loyal to the old royal line were able to defeat the forces of Amon. Hatshepsut was crowned Pharaoh and Tuthmose III was sent off to Nubia.

Now the obelisks had arrived, and where better to put them than squarely in the middle of the hall of Tuthmose I where Amon had, with a certain amount of priestly assistance, selected despised Tuthmose III?

These obelisks at Karnak were ordered by Hatshepsut, whose inscription urges the wondering visitor to think, "How like her it is!"

Off came the roof of Tuthmose I's hall, down came all the cedar columns in its southern half, down came four of the cedar columns in the northern half, down came the entire south wall so that the obelisks might be brought in and put in place. Then Hatshepsut, quite content, returned to her palace and, from time to time, looked out with satisfaction of a bright and beamish morning to see her electrum points gleaming brightly in the rays of Ra.

Until, that is, Tuthmose III came back and Hatshepsut disappeared. Then a spite fence of stone, sufficiently high to conceal the obelisks from the eyes of the visitor standing below, was erected by Pharaoh. His hated half sister's monuments disappeared from sight until some centuries later when time and attrition revealed them again to public view. Now one lies fallen and one stands proudly exposed. It is still taller than one erected by Tuthmose I. And none at all of Tuthmose III's survives at Karnak. Thirty-five hundred years later, sweet Hatshepsut has the final word. Inscribed on the base of the standing obelisk is a description of its creation and the admonition: "Let not him who hears this say that what I have said is a lie, but rather let him say, 'How like her it is!'"

She also shares with her father the distinction of being the only obelisk builders — a favorite pastime of the Eighteenth and Nineteenth Dynasties — to have all their obelisks still in Egypt. During the merry period of plunder that fell upon

helpless Egypt in the nineteenth century of the Christian era, one of Tuthmose III's obelisks went to Constantinople, one to London, one to Rome, where it stands in front of the church of St. John Lateran, and one to New York where, for reasons unknown to Tuthmose, it is known as "Cleopatra's Needle." Ramesses II, overdoing obelisks as he did everything else, created so many of them that nobody has an exact count. Fourteen at least were erected by him at Tanis in the Delta, two more at Luxor, others at as yet undiscovered sites. But, inevitably, three of his are in Rome, and one of the two from Luxor is in Paris. Everybody wanted a piece of the Egyptian action in those days, and Egypt was powerless to protest...

Sights seen — the long dusty corniche of Aswan explored, god Horus fended off in his bumbling near-collision with the balcony at the Oberoi — and the day plunges headlong toward the rapid African night. Now is the time to experience Ancient Egypt in the most intimate and characteristic way it can be experienced: on the water.

They are young, the felucca pilots, they are Nubian, and they are merry. They know the Nile with unerring instinct born of a simple fact: they have been on it, and in it, since they were old enough to walk. Older brothers have younger brothers riding with them — or sometimes younger cousins — in that endless network of familial relationships in the eastern world that runs from river to farm to bazaar to hotel to market place to government office to airport to everywhere. Somebody is always related to somebody. Somebody always knows somebody who can sell you such-and-such — "for a very good price."

Everybody sticks together in a long, unending chain, a defense against loneliness, a defense against hunger, a defense against want and the uncertain challenges of the modern world. Felucca pilots beget felucca pilots, older train younger; the sails are neatly furled when going downriver, there is a scramble up the mast to unfurl them when a breeze blows upriver; sometimes, when Hapi refuses any wind at all, there is the simple backbreaking labor of rowing. But the craft they manage descends from the most ancient times, and its affinity with the river is as absolute and unbreakable as their own. They know Hapi's every mood and he knows theirs. As long as both observe their timeless compact, all is well.

There are feluccas in Cairo, too, but the Nile is too broad and too active there as it hurries to the sea for any kind of serenity or association with the past. The traffic roars, the commercial boats chug back and forth; peace eludes. Upper Egypt is the place to know the Nile; and in Aswan, as in Luxor, the hour or so between the start of Ra's decline and his final swift farewell as he disappears into the cavern of the west, there to begin his nightlong journey underground back to the east again, is the hour in which to do it.

Now the river turns golden, then bronze, then slate as Ra descends. The distant hum of the waterfront, such as it is in Aswan and Luxor, becomes more distant. Across the water comes laughter from another felucca, a jocular greeting, the slap of sails in the lightly rising breeze. Along the bank straight-backed, black-

Felucca pilots know the Nile's every mood and the Nile knows theirs. As long as both observe their timeless compact, all is well.

swathed young women, faces often hidden in the Muslim style but eyes sparkling and gurgles of laughter and ribald comment unexpectedly breaking out, emerge from the darkening, neat-kept fields to come down through the rushes to fill the water jugs they carry upon their stately heads. Farther along, men and boys strip, dive in, lather up, rinse off, drink deep. Bilharzia lives in many places in these waters and some suffer from it. But most know the areas to avoid and treat the Nile for what it is: their highway, trade route, bathtub, water-provider, life-giver, protector, friend.

One moves slowly among the grotesque rocks of Elephantine at Aswan, slowly along the placid fields of the western bank at Luxor: twilight, once begun, moves fast. It grows darker and more silent, the river glow begins to fade, pilots and passengers alike become more thoughtful. Distantly in imagined memory come the blare of trumpets, the splash of oars of great, gold-painted barges, the gleam of flares upon the water: face to the west, eyes upon Ra as he disappears from sight, Pharaoh is passing. Five thousand years of history are going by. This is how it feels now: one knows with unshakable certainty that this is how it felt then. Past and present fuse, become one. Nothing has changed, the river is eternal, it is all exactly the same.

Ra goes, the dark encloses; slowly the felucca swings around and heads back toward the lights, the tourists, the hotel, the cocktail hour, and dinner. But in the mind, it does not change. Hapi has cast his spell of five thousand years. Once felt, it will not be forgotten, living in the heart, companion to the *ka*.

Ancient tombs and an ancient temple
dominate the west bank at Aswan.

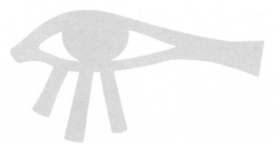

*The river's peace at Aswan carries
late boaters home.*

No priests, acolytes, worshippers
remain. Only the stones, the palms,
the fragments that once housed a
powerful and avaricious god bear
witness on the western bank.

All through their long history, Hapi's children paid him heartfelt tribute. Two of the most typical:

From the Pyramid Texts, Fifth and Sixth Dynasties, c. 2750—2475 B.C.—

They tremble, that behold the Nile in full flood. The fields laugh and the riverbanks are overflowed. The god's offerings descend, the visage of men is bright, and the heart of the gods rejoices.

From the Nineteenth Dynasty, c. 1359—1205 B.C.—

Praise to you, O Nile, who issue from the earth and come to nourish Egypt: you who water the meadows, you that Ra has created to nourish all cattle, who gives drink to the desert places that are far from water . . . you who makes barley and creates wheat, so that you may cause the temples to flourish . . .

If you be sluggish, the nostrils are stopped up and all men are impoverished; the victuals of the gods are diminished and millions of men perish . . . (When you withhold yourself) the whole land is in terror and great and small lament. When you rise, the land is in exultation and everybody is in joy. All jaws begin to laugh and every tooth is revealed . . .

You that brings victuals and are rich in food, who creates all that is good . . . who creates herbage for the cattle . . . who fills the storehouses and makes wide the granaries, who gives things to the poor . . . who makes trees to grow according to every wish . . .

Your young folk and your children shout for joy over you, and men hail you as king . . . you that vomits forth, giving the fields to drink and making strong the people . . . you light that comes from the darkness . . . you that comes with splendid things and adorns the earth . . . you that makes green the Two Riverbanks.

You are verdant, O Nile, you are verdant, you that makes man to live on his cattle and his cattle on the meadow.

You are verdant, you are verdant; O Nile, you are verdant.

It was a good day to drive down the river from Aswan to Luxor—almost any day in Egypt is a good day, although in Luxor one gray morning it actually rained for a few minutes, first such sprinkle in many months—and both the countryside and two major temples make the journey worthwhile. In the river villages life proceeds unchanged in direct descent from pharaonic times. People are somewhat differently dressed, perhaps, since the Ancients did not bother much with clothing and usually went naked about the temples, fields and towns except in chilly weather or at times of ceremony or special occasion. To be clothed all the time is a convention that came later, with conquerors and the establishment of the Muslim religion. In a climate that ninety percent of the year ranges from hot to very hot, nakedness was natural. Besides, who cared? Pharaoh appeared clothed for ceremony, but in his palaces—and in Akhenaten's case, occasionally in public—he and his family were as casual as the rest.

Nowadays, of course, the gelabaya for men, the gracefully falling folds of black for women, are virtually standard in the villages, mixed increasingly with western dress as one moves farther downriver toward Cairo. But even there and in such other major cities as Alexandria, Minya, Assiut, flowing whites and blacks provide a pleasant mix with the business suits, slacks, jeans and sport shirts of the West.

If one takes the grand tour by Nile steamer from Aswan to Luxor, a most pleasant way to do it, one spends five nights on the boat and three actually moving on the river, tying up each night along the way. An illusion of movement is maintained, but it is geared pretty closely to the pharaonic pace. The prices are also pharaonic.

The drive takes approximately six hours with a break for lunch. The cost is minimal compared to the boat, and one becomes a participant in the swarming life of modern Egypt rather than a deck-chair observer.

So we went by car, starting around ten in the morning, most of the time in sight of the river, through small villages and larger towns, honking our way through that characteristic conglomeration of adults, children, donkeys, camels, cattle, horse carts, automobiles of uncertain vintage, pack-jammed foul-belching buses, people, people, people, that one sees everywhere in Mideast, Africa and Orient from Morocco on through India to Hong Kong. The pattern is always the same: the swarm, the flowing tide, the blowing horn, the waves parting momentarily to let one through, the near escapes, the grazed shins, the scraped fenders, the noisy imprecations or the skeptical, appraising glances, the tide closing impassively behind as though one had never been. Here you realize modern Egypt's population problem: that narrow strip of green supports almost forty million people, increasing at an estimated rate of a million a year; and unless Lake Nasser, far to the south between Aswan and Abu Simbel, can be given sufficient irrigation canals to bring the water many hundreds of miles north—or unless the Qattara Depression in the northwestern

In small villages along the Nile, essentially unchanged since ancient days, modern Egypt's population climbs steadily toward a number the narrow valley can barely support.

desert near Cairo can indeed be filled, as some planners dream, with desalinated sea water—then very serious trouble lies ahead.

(In the airport at Abu Simbel a pleasant-faced engineer fell to talking while we waited for the plane: he and his colleagues were constructing a canal there some three hundred miles long out into the Nubian plain. The hope was to bring many thousands of acres under irrigation and development. But, he said, eyes widening in thought, there was no way of telling whether the people would go out there and farm it, unless forcibly required to do so, which is not the way of present Egypt. They mostly seemed to prefer to stay closer to the river. . .)

We came, in an hour or so, to the temple of Kom Ombo, a relative new-comer to Egypt's relics—Ptolemaic, built some time after 330 B.C., its walls covered with hieroglyphics which had become so esoteric by that time that some of them still cannot be translated with any certainty. It stands on a commanding elevation overlooking the river, the cultivated plain and the Red Land just beyond; in ruins, but the ruins well preserved and a major portion of them being gradually restored.

It was devoted to the worship of Se-bek, the crocodile god; and Sebek is as good an example as any of that baffling and often not exactly understandable pred-ilection of the Ancients for making their religion just as confusing as possible—to us, that is. They seemed to have no trouble at all knowing what they were about. It is only the ignorant barbarians with their cameras from beyond the Great Green who have the difficulty.

Sebek, to the modern glance, would not seem to be a particularly friendly god. Crocodiles are not very nice characters—even though one is assured very confidently from Aswan north that there are no more in the river, that they are all now south behind the High Dam, that they have been extirpated from there all the way to Cairo. And of course the Egyptians do swim in the river, and apparently quite freely, and a few of them on occasion are observed to be hardy enough to swim all the way across; and nothing happens—as far as the visitor knows. Officially, the word is: no more Sebeks in Upper and Lower Egypt; still some, presumably, in wretched Kush.

But now observe the Ancients and the way they regarded Sebek. Sebek was a good guy. His favorable reputation (which overlooked a lot of Egyptians who must have found themselves eaten, down through the centuries) dated back to the great battle in the beginning of creation between the god O-si-ris, lord of death and the afterworld, and his evil brother Set, who battled him so furiously (after Set tried to wrest Egypt from him) that Set finally tore Osiris into pieces and scattered him along the Nile. Osiris' sister-wife, Isis, aided by her sister Nephthys, found the pieces and put them back together again (vividly pictured at the cow-goddess Hat-hor's temple of Dendera, north of Luxor, where the viewer is left in no doubt whatsoever that Osiris' manly virility was indeed thoroughly restored). Sebek, presumably because he lived in the Nile and knew, so to speak, where the body was buried, was able to assist Isis in her revivifying task. Therefore he became associated with the restoration of Osiris' life; therefore he became associated with all restoration of life; therefore one of the deadliest beasts on earth became, for the Ancient Egyptian, a symbol of life.

Similarly Set, a villain in some parts of the country, was worshipped in others; and when Ramesses I's son came to the throne he took the name Seti, apparently in his honor. Yet when he built the beautiful temple of Abydos in honor of Osiris, he carefully had the figure of Set removed from his oval cartouches, or nameplates, on the temple walls and substituted the figure of Osiris instead.

So you see how easy Egyptian mythology is, and how consistently and rationally, by our standards, the Ancients treated it—if you just pay attention very, ve-rrry closely. This becomes that, that becomes this, up is down and down is up; and usually the head of some animal or bird is tacked on top. It is best to just ride with it and not try to understand it too thoroughly; although, when we get to Luxor, we'll give it a try.

Anyway, there does exist, at Kom Ombo, a separate room, one of several that originally existed when the temple was at its height, filled to the top with mummified crocodiles. They grin out at the visitor across two thousand years, through the heavy meshed wire that protects them from the modern souvenir-hunter, with a certain savage humor. *You* think we're deadly, they seem to be saying, but there was a time around here when we had it made. Tough for you if you hadn't respected us then, boy. You could have been tossed to us in the river. *Then* you'd have found out what kind of symbol of life we were.

On down the road, after one passes through a roadside village market swarming with the produce and the people of miles around, one comes at last to one of the most impressive of all Egypt's relics, the Temple of Horus. Horus of Edfu is still one of the most alive of all the great gods, and it is with some feeling of lingering genuine respect that the sensitive visitor enters his precincts now.

Here at Edfu was the center of the worship of the hawk-headed god most closely identified with Pharaoh. Horus was the son of Osiris. Somehow over the centuries Pharaoh became identified with both of them. When he died he too became Osiris, but while he lived he was Horus. Therefore "the Living Horus" was another of his regular titles, along with Lord of the Two Lands, King of the North and South, Lord of Diadems, Mighty Bull, Son of the Sun.

Others were added from time to time by individual Pharaohs—there was always room for one more. The six above are the principal and most consistent down the millennia.

Here behind the great walls, now called pylons, that form the front entrance, one walks into an open courtyard to be confronted by one of the most striking portrayals of all the gods—the sculpture of Horus, perhaps five feet tall, on a pedestal that raises him yet taller, flanking the entrance to the temple's inner mysteries. Two of him once stood there, identical; the one that remains is quite impressive enough. Two must have cowed the most brash of supplicants.

The temple of Kom Ombo, sacred to the crocodile god Sebek, presides serenely over the river on the way from Aswan to Luxor.

His mien is majestic, his expression severe. There is no nonsense about Horus of Edfu, even though there were some high old times in the temple in the old days. He was married to Hathor, a rather unlikely union of falcon and cow—but again, it made sense to the Ancients—and once a year her priests and priestesses brought her up the river from Dendera, past Thebes to Edfu, there to enjoy her reunion with her husband while the priests and priestesses enjoyed *their* reunions with the priests and priestesses of Horus. It was all very religious, but one can't keep up the rituals and ceremonies *every* hour of the day. There comes a time...

So, once a year, all was very merry in the Temple of Edfu, while Horus, his expression eternally disapproving, looked on. Afterwards, there were many solemn propitiary gestures and much tribute placed at his feet and in the inner sanctum; and everybody in Edfu stood on the riverbank and waved wistfully to the great barge of Hathor and her exhausted attendants as they went happily, if somewhat blearily, back down the river to Dendera. Whether Pharaoh ever attended one of these ceremonies, discovered records do not tell; but there is no doubt that it served as a good safety valve for the priesthoods of Horus and Hathor, and for the population that flocked in thousands from all over Upper Egypt. In the same fashion the great feast of Opet at Thebes—the grandest community drunk in Ancient Egypt—honored Amon and simultaneously released a lot of tensions that might otherwise have threatened Pharaoh and the priesthood.

Drinking and the big celebration, in fact, were major features of Ancient Egyptian life. Because of the fascination with funerary rites, a gloomy pall has been cast over the land in the minds of many later observers; but the purpose of the rites is thus misunderstood. This was a basically happy and optimistic people, despite the many ups and downs of their long national life. They were so concerned with getting everything exactly right when they died because they felt that if everything was, then the afterlife would be just as jolly as this. Their famous set of funerary instructions was unfortunately given by early scholars the title which will always adhere to it: *The Book of the Dead*. But to the Ancients it was known as *The Book of Coming Forth by Day* (from the tomb), which is quite a different matter: a guidebook to the pleasant afterworld in the West, and many busy hints and instructions as how to best make one's way there and enjoy it to the utmost.

Certainly the Ancients enjoyed their earthly life to the utmost, every chance they got. Not only at the great festivals such as those of Edfu and Opet, but at banquets and dinners from Pharaoh's Great House on down the social scale to the peasants in the villages relaxing after a hard day's work in the fields, everybody loved singing, dancing, and a good jug—often many—of beer or wine. References to drunkenness abound in the texts, and among the paintings in the tombs are many that show citizens who have imbibed quite a bit too much. One lady, in fact, is shown turning away from the table to be delicately sick into a basin patiently held by a handmaiden. After the battle of Megiddo the scribe notes of Tuthmose III's troops in their moment of triumph: "Behold, the army of his Majesty was drunk and

Down the long corridors of the temple of Kom Ombo the priests and worshippers of Sebek, the crocodile god, paid tribute to their fearsome deity.

78

anointed with oil as at a feast in Egypt." Anointing with oil was another jovial custom. Usually the oil was contained in a conical cap of beeswax placed on the head. As the evening advanced, the wine flowed and the party grew more merry, the wax melted, the scented oil dripped over the body, and things became even more pleasant than they were already.

Today, of course, the very distant inheritors of these jolly souls pay the usual Muslim tribute to the ban on liquor in their religion. Like Mormons, some do and some don't. Liquor is available in the major hotels and restaurants, flows freely in private homes of a certain economic level, and even the poor have occasional access to beer and wine. The truly devout won't touch it, and many do not; the more practical work out a reasonable accommodation between the demands of Mohammed and the solace of the grape and its stronger companions. Public drunkenness is virtually unknown, however, and it seems safe to say that the modern Egyptians are a long way from the apparently quite universal carousing that often sent the Ancients happily reeling.

One walks the corridors of Edfu, best preserved of all the temples—originally built, it is assumed, by the famous Im-ho-tep, architect to King Zoser of the Third Dynasty and builder of the Step Pyramid, and restored in Ptolemaic times to the structure standing today—with a little of the serenity that must have rested upon it in the long months between Hathor's festivals. It is quiet place, save for the morning hour or so when the Nile boat stops and its tourists swarm ashore, or when some busload of earnest Germans or French descends upon it. White-gelabayaed figures appear and disappear here and there among the dimly lit rooms; now and again one ubiquitously offers a candle to illuminate some item of special interest. The inner sanctum, like that of Amon, is quiet, dark, and secret. Emerging into the sunlight again, one sees Horus frowning fiercely by the door, and knows that there has never been any doubt as to who was in charge here.

Not that he achieved his eminence easily, however: his bad old Uncle Set was after him, too. When Isis, with the help of Sebek and a few others, had put dismembered Osiris back together again, Osiris was dead but she still managed to conceive a child by him. The child was Horus, and as Osiris' heir he had the right to rule Egypt. But Set had not given up. A papyrus from the reign of Ramesses V of the Twentieth Dynasty discloses that Set went to considerable lengths to discredit his nephew. Ra-Atum, the greatest god of truly ancient, pre-Amon times, and his fellow senior gods sat in judgment on their dispute and finally ordered them to stop quarreling. Wily Set appeared to agree and suggested companionably to Horus, "Come on, let's have a good time in my house!"

"And Horus said to him, 'I'll do it; certainly, I'll be most glad to do it!'

"And so when evening came, the bed was spread for them, and the two of them lay down together. And then in the night Set made his penis stiff and he thrust it between the thighs of Horus. But Horus put his hands between his thighs and caught the semen of Set."

Sebek, in the mysterious and sometimes baffling rationale of the Ancients' religion, became not a deadly beast but a symbol and protector of life.

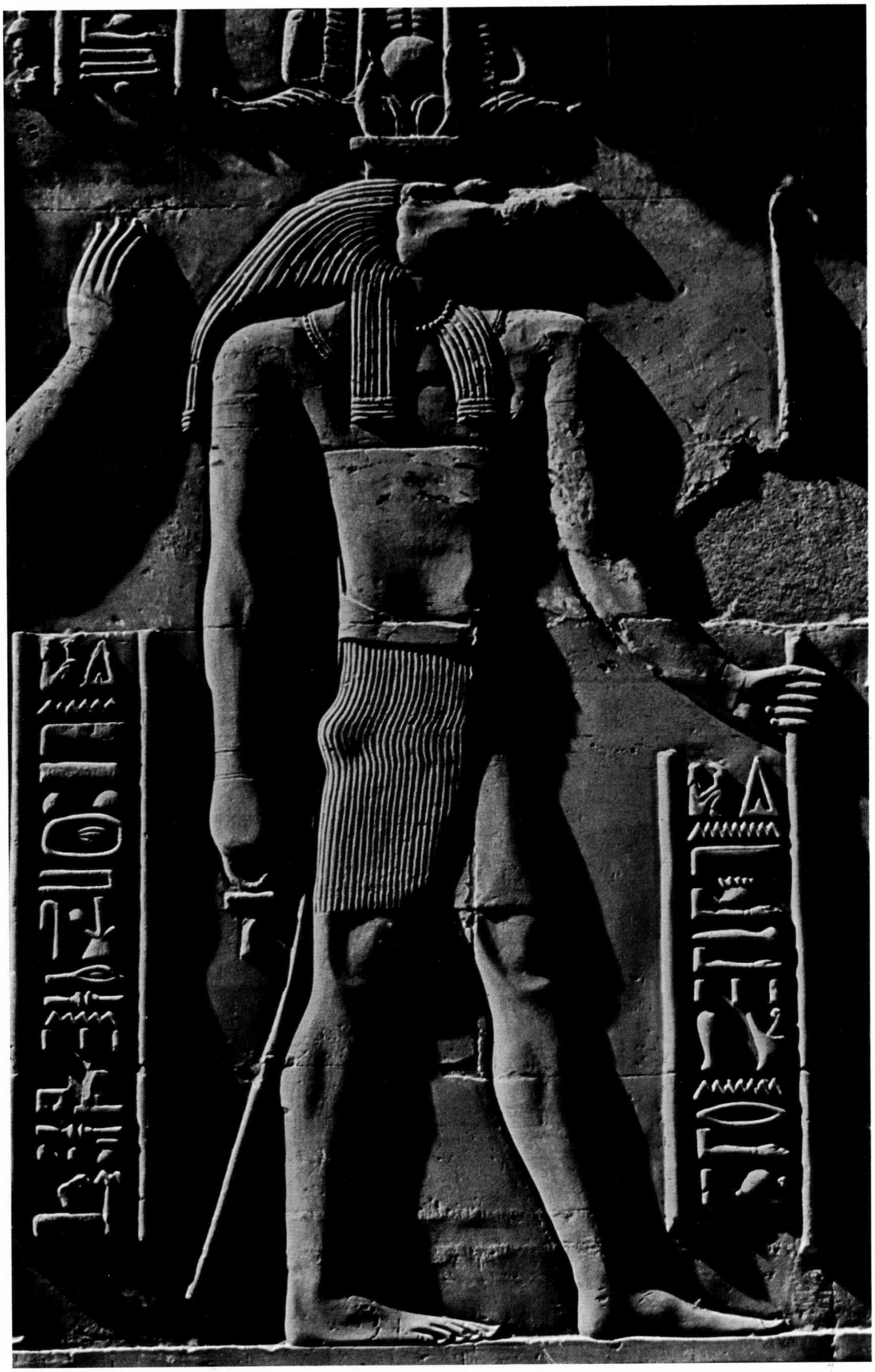

One of the best preserved of all temples, that of the falcon god Horus at Edfu, greets the visitor. Horus stands at the gate, looking fierce; but he allows the respectful to come in.

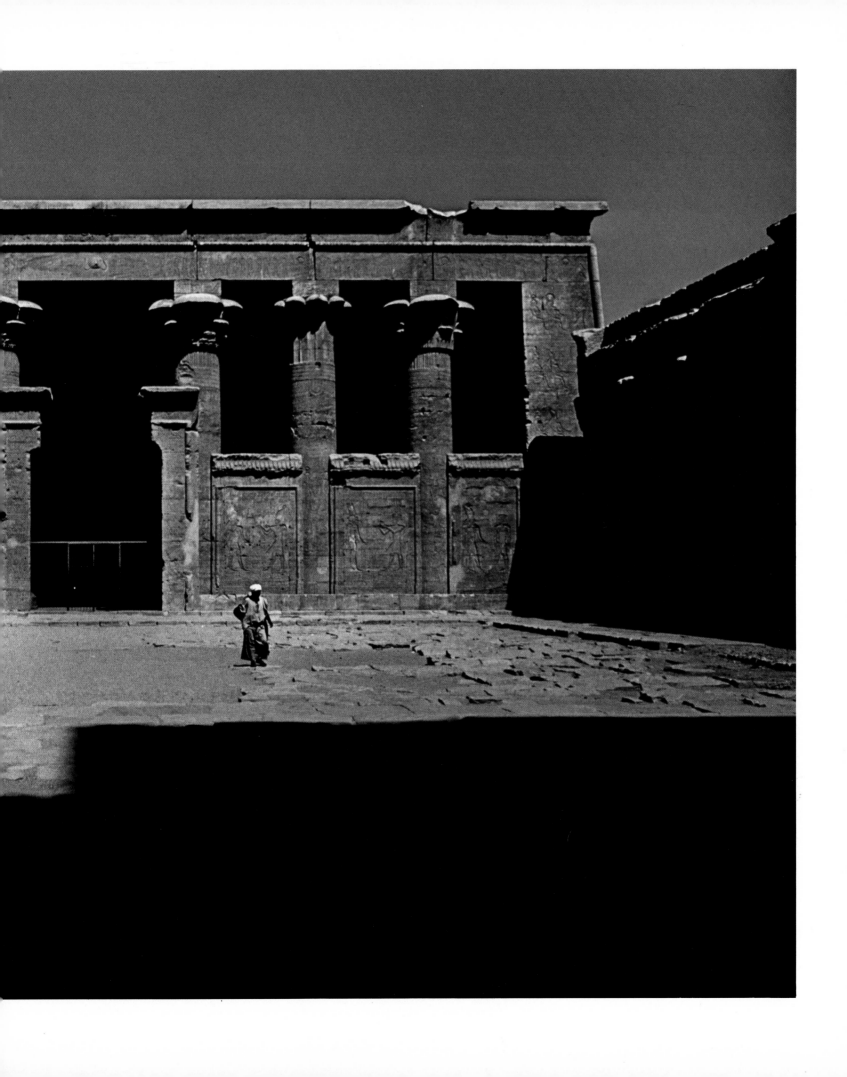

At Edfu, as at most other temples, pharaoh after pharaoh recorded his life and triumphs down the long sun-blasted corridors.

He then carried Set's semen to his mother. Isis gave a loud cry and cut off both his hands—but, being a good mother, she promptly replaced them with two clean ones. She then determined to take drastic measures. She assisted Horus to produce his own semen, which she put on Set's lettuce (lettuce being still considered an aphrodisiac in Egypt today). Unaware of this, Set ate his lettuce and promptly became pregnant by Horus. At this point Ra-Atum and his colleagues finally got fed up with all this nonsense and demanded that the semen of Horus come forth from Set, which it did in the form of a golden sun-disk that appeared on Set's head, annoying him considerably. (He was further annoyed when Thoth promptly stole it and put it on *his* head.)

Eventually, after many more adventures, during which Set tore out one of Horus' eyes—the so-called *wadjet-eye* which is still a major good-luck charm in Egypt—Horus was declared heir of Osiris and rightful ruler of Egypt.

Things like that aren't easy for a fellow to take, though—they can mark him for life. It is no wonder, perhaps, that Horus looks so severe to this very day.

How seriously the Ancients took this kind of story, with its long, involved fantasies and its sudden startling crudities, it is hard to determine now. Atum, for instance, original god on earth, is declared quite frankly to have masturbated to produce his god-son and goddess-daughter, who in turn created the other leading gods of the pantheon. Hathor is described as having gone on a rampage at one time, killing everyone she met in her way, until she was cured of this when wine was put in her path and she got so drunk she forgot all about it and became the amiable goddess of the standard texts. Only two of the gods seem to have escaped this sometimes surprising humanization, and they, significantly enough, were the god who developed the most stern and powerful priesthood, Amon; and the god who won the allegiance of a revolutionary pharaoh, the Aten. The rest abound in human foibles, which apparently did not disturb their ancient worshippers. As with the Greek and Roman gods of later times, they seem to have been regarded as larger-than-life people, with all that this implies for ethical and moral behavior.

In one of the rooms, thrown into wavering relief by the light of a candle (its uncertain rays followed by the inevitable request for baksheesh, which is a burden some tourists resent but should not, for it is often the only money the attendants make), is the famous panel of surgical instruments upon which, together with certain medical texts, are based the scholarly legend and the popular assumption that the Ancient Egyptians were greatly advanced in the practice of medicine. They were not. They deserve attention for many things, but medicine is not one of them. They understood something about trepanning, they had some knowledge of setting broken limbs, they were able to extract a painful tooth (though Amonhotep III is believed to have suffered miserably from abscesses and infections his doctors could not cure). But the great bulk of their medicine was pure and simple magic. Typical is a spell for getting rid of a headache which appeals to a great number of the gods for help:

"O Ra, O Atum, O Shu, O Geb, O Nut, O Anubis who is before the divine

Horus' uncle, the god Set, gave him a hard time when he was a boy; he looks as though he hasn't quite gotten over it, yet.

shrine, O Horus, O Set, O Isis, O Nephthys, O Great Ennead, O Little Ennead, come and see your father who enters clothed in radiance to see the horn of Sekhmet! Come remove that enemy, dead man or dead woman, male foe or female foe, who is in the face of So-and-so, born of the woman So-and-So!"

This is to be recited over a crocodile made of clay, grain in its mouth, a faience eye in its head. The prayer should be tied in a drawing of the gods on fine linen and should be placed on the head of the sufferer. Or, alternatively, it can be recited over an image of Ra, Atum, Shu, Mehyt, Geb, Nut, Anubis, Horis, Set, Isis, Nephthys and Anoryx, with a figure carrying a spear standing on the back of the sufferer. By that time, presumably, the sufferer will be so fascinated by all this that he will have forgotten about his headache.

Most of Ancient Egypt's so-called "medicine" is the same. It was not a science and it relied heavily on magic and the will of the gods. If they agreed, the patient got well. If they did not, that was his hard luck and there wasn't much the physicians could do about it.

From Edfu the road continues north toward Luxor past the site of el-Kab, capital of Upper Egypt in the time of Menes. There are the ruins of its great wall—an empty plain within—memories of the most ancient days—nothing else to hold the traveler. Farms and villages, and now and again, in the low, accompanying cliff along the river, a row of rectangular dark holes, mysterious, uncommunicative, aloof: tombs of the very ancient, mostly Old and Middle Kingdoms, opened and plundered many, many centuries ago, the mummies and jewels of their Amhoteps, Imhoteps, Ke-gem-nes, Ptah-ho-teps and the rest scattered and lost, probably forever, in the secretive sands of Egypt.

Away from the river for a time, then back again; and finally in the distance a higher range, already beginning to turn faintly purple in the slanting rays of late afternoon. Increasing cultivation, increasing traffic, increasing livestock and human-ity. Suddenly the back streets of a sizable town, a quick glimpse of distant colonnades off to the right, and into a tree-shaded street along the Nile. Feluccas tied up along the riverbank, a huge temple on the left, across the river in the declining light a high pointed peak with many rocky ridges trailing down from it—the "Peak of the West," the royal necropolis—and Luxor, ancient Thebes, heart of the ancient world.

Luxor is in many ways the most charming city in Egypt, partly because history is everywhere, partly because Nubians provide an amiable and needed leaven, partly because the whole pace of life is slower, easier, gentler than it is anywhere else in the Two Lands, even Aswan. In, around, above, beneath, is ancient Thebes. It reaches out to touch one everywhere: modern Luxor is here, one feels, almost on sufferance. Time has paused in this place and never quite started up again. More and more of the past is being uncovered, protected, restored to some semblance of its original overpowering impact. Here the Ancients live as nowhere else; and here the timeless flow of the river and the unending history of Egypt, winding out of the past like the Nile itself, out of the most ancient days into now and on into the unforeseeable future, control the tempo, the moods and the very conditions of life itself, for both visitor and native.

In Luxor, if one has the time—and the traveler who wishes to get the most out of the experience would be well advised to arrange it so that he does have the time, four days at the least, a week if it can be managed—one finds oneself relaxing immediately into the casual pace of things. The horse carriages rattle past along the waterfront or stand strategically waiting at every corner and hotel entrance, their drivers calling out, "See Karnak? See city? See museum?" and doing quite well with it, furnishing a reasonably priced ride—if one bargains beforehand and is firm about it. There are official signs requesting, for humanitarian reasons, that passengers not encourage their drivers to race the horses. They are not always observed by all tourists or all drivers, but by most. Nile tourist steamers are anchored at intervals along the bank, ranging from the most modern to older types full of age, atmosphere and things both edible and verminous of which the traveler had best be fully aware and extremely cautious. Feluccas are anchored in neat rows between them, their grinning young drivers shouting up to the passing stranger, touting the glories of a ride on the Nile or a trip to Banana Island, where, as the name implies, there are bananas, plus other things of which the tourist should also be cautious and aware. Along the corniche the donkeys trot, uttering their eternal agonized complaints, drawing carts heavy-laden with produce, driven by small boys who seem barely old enough to walk, let alone have that much responsibility.

Two blocks from the hotels the busy main street, lined with tiny shops, most handling just a single item, surges day and night with life. Closer by, in the arcade between the Winter Palace Hotel and Amonhotep III's massive Luxor Temple, the antique dealers have their shops. Some state honestly: "Excellent Reproductions." Others are officially licensed by the government—or claim to be—and assert that everything they have is authentic. Still others have owners who strike a balance calculated to lower the guard of the buyer by saying with a great show of candor: "This is fake—this is fake—this is fake—*that* is real—*that* is real—*that* is real." Probably the best and most reliable of all Egypt's antique dealers, Eliah Nassar of Nassar Brothers in Khan el-Kalili Bazaar in Cairo, sums it up this way: "Mr. Drury, there are people up the river who know more about making instant antiques than you

Modern Luxor awakes in the rising light of Ra in the morning; but here in the heart of what was ancient Thebes, the temple of Luxor still dominates the riverbank as it has done for more than three thousand years.

It is still very early, but already the day is beginning on the broad swift-flowing waters of the river that was deified under the name Hapi. Hapi's children, today as always, set out in the mists of morning to begin their commerce.

and I and Mr. Carter and Mr. Begin and Mr. Sadat, all put together, will ever know about anything." But with considerable caution, a lot of thought, a genuine interest and some comparative knowledge, it is possible now and then to find something really unusual and genuine in Luxor. The things are there, under all the dust: not many, nowadays, but some.

Across the river in the necropolis the people of the village of el-Qurna, like their ancestors for the better part of five thousand years, are still burrowing away; and now and again they find something, and sooner or later it appears in a shop. Pharaonic governments tried without success for millennia to control the grave robbers of the West Bank. The government of today tries just as hard, with somewhat better success, but it does not succeed entirely. Grave-robbing is still a way of life, and it is quite likely that the village elders who run el-Qurna with an iron hand still know more about what lies beneath the rocks of the necropolis than the Organization of Antiquities and all the earnest young archeological expeditions from Poland, Germany, France and the universities of Chicago, Pennsylvania and Toronto, combined.

In addition to the shops of the arcade, there are also the persistent men and youths who approach the visitor beside the Luxor Temple, at Karnak, or along the riverbank. From the folds of the gelabaya, wrapped in dirty old scraps of newspaper, come big scarabs, little scarabs, heads of Nefertiti, shards of pottery, necklaces of mummy beads, delicately worked heads on sandstone slabs that "my father got off the wall of the temple." If they were genuine, as one carriage driver remarked scornfully after a clamoring group of eight or ten had proffered these wares, they would be worth six hundred pounds instead of the twenty or thirty asked. If the visitor is interested—and some of the work is very fine, and not all that many back in Kansas City will have the knowledge to challenge it anyway—it is possible to get these for one or two pounds—if one bargains. One always bargains: it is a way of life.

Food in Egypt, aside from the major hotels and some few special restaurants in Cairo, Alexandria and Luxor, is generally not so enjoyable for the tourist. It is heavy on rice, lamb, fresh vegetables that look fine but must be approached with care; usually overcooked fish; and beef that is not always beef but sometimes water buffalo. Liquor is very high in the hotels, cheap in the occasional bottle shop along the street if one is not fussy about brands and also desperate for a drink. Beer is potable, wines are monotonous but not bad. In Luxor, unless one chooses the restaurant atop the arcade, one dines in the company of enormous, quick-skim, in-and-out tourist groups at the Winter Palace, the Etap or the Savoy. Aside from the arcade restaurant, dining is perhaps the only aspect of life in Luxor that is not leisurely and relaxed.

But so much else is that it doesn't matter much; and when the visitor is fortunate enough to have his first night in Luxor coincide with the *Sound and Light* at Karnak, all else falls away.

The sprint is desperate, the goal is baksheesh. Now, as always, Hapi's youngsters seek their fortunes along the riverbank.

God Ra rises over Luxor and the site of Thebes where he was worshipped for more than two millennia. Soon the city will be roaring with people, cars, horse carriages, donkeys, camels, goats, dogs, chickens—all the life that has gone on in this place essentially unchanged from the farthest reaches of recorded time.

Now Ra, too, has had his day;
and as the land, exhausted from the
heat, sinks slowly to rest along with
its people, he prepares to descend
beneath the earth in the west, there to
enter his sacred barque and make his
nighttime journey back under the
earth so that he may rise again in
the east and bless his worshippers
anew tomorrow.

"Welcome, O traveler to Upper Egypt," says the pleasant feminine voice. "You are about to enter the House of the Father." But it is more than the House of Father Amon that the traveler is about to enter. It is the heart and essence of all that distant and mystic world, which here is close, immediate and alive, of Ancient Egypt.

You can see them now along the Nile. We are in Thebes in the greatest days of the Eighteenth Dynasty. The capital is vibrant with activity from the Temple of Luxor in the center of the city to the Temple of Karnak two miles north along the river. From the great entrance pylons of both, bright flags are flying in the restless little breeze that is cooling Thebes this day. Great figures of Pharaoh and the gods stride across the front of the pylons; in and out between their massive stone abutments passes a steady stream of priests, supplicants, worshippers, government officials. Hapi's broad expanse is covered with shipping, hand-rown boats, larger, graceful feluccas, big, ponderous barges that have anchored after their long journey up from the Delta or the shorter trip down from the First Cataract. Those from the Delta are filled with cattle, grain, produce of the villages, cedars from Lebanon, fine goods and textiles, gold and other tribute from Syria and the city-states of nearer Asia and the shores of the Great Green. Those from the First Cataract carry slaves, gold from the mines of Nubia, incense and myrrh and unusual woods and plants from Punt.

Along the waterfront stand the palaces of the pharaohs, not built of stone as are the temples of the gods, but of mud brick like the commonest hovel of the commonest herdsman in the village. But unlike his modest dwelling, the interior walls of the palaces are covered with vivid paintings of members of the royal family engaged in such pleasant pastimes as hunting and fishing. Thick rugs cover the earthen floors, linen draperies frame the doorways, kept open during the day and frequently at night to allow a free flow of air.

The palace complex at this moment contains some of the walls of Hatshepsut's palace, appropriated and absorbed—of course—into the walls of Tuthmose III's; the palaces of Amonhotep I and II, and a very small, very old portion, weathered down to a few rounded fragments off in one corner, of the palace of Ahmose I, conqueror of the Hyksos, founder of the dynasty. Around the lot runs a continuous mud wall, perhaps ten feet in height, its level top interrupted at regular intervals by watchtowers and guardhouses. There are two main entryways, also carefully guarded, through which pass a bustling, unending stream of government officials ranging from the lowest clerks to the highest dignitaries. This particular palace complex is used now to house the offices of the Vizier of the South and other high officials, the Overseer of Pharaoh's Works, the commander of the armies, Pharaoh's sculptor, and the like.

Pharaoh himself, Amonhotep III, has built his palace where no other pharaoh ever has or ever will again—on the West Bank, south of the necropolis, near the region of the dead. His people have never quite understood this, and he of course has not been under any necessity to explain his decision to anyone. It is simply his will; and Pharaoh's will now, as always in days of glory, is supreme over all.

Except, possibly, the busy priests of Amon who scurry in and out of the two huge temples like so many ceaseless ants. In those two places—and particularly at

Karnak—they preside over a machinery almost as vast and far-reaching as Pharaoh's own. There are farms and villages to be administered, great herds of cattle, mines, shipyards, granaries; all the enormous wealth of Amon's state-within-a-state. Here Pharaoh comes to worship the god on set occasions. It is significant that he comes to Amon—Amon does not come to him. He cannot enter until he has been properly received by the High Priest and all has been made suitably ready. God is worshipping god. He is in the house of *his* father, Amon; and only the malformed child Amonhotep IV, soon to become Akhenaten, has any qualms about this on this pleasant day.

Elsewhere in Thebes are the shops, the bazaars, the mud-brick homes and hovels, all the bustling ongoing life that exists in Luxor today. The only difference is that the men, women and children who walk through the streets to stop or chat are shorter, browner, more scantily clad; and items on the shelves or spread out on rugs before the purchaser are less fancy, diverse and complicated. The basic staples of bread, meat, vegetables, beer, wine, are just the same, on this day we are visiting 3,200 years ago.

Across the teeming river, filled with all the far-flung commerce of the empire, much busier now than it will be long after when the capital is far to the north in Cairo, there can be seen the painted colonnades and brilliant standards of the mortuary temples of several of the pharaohs who have gone before. The small temple of Amonhotep I and Tuthmose III, forerunner of Medinet Habu, can be distantly ascertained. Hatshepsut's Deir el-Bahri gleams low, white and perfect against the barren cliffs. Alongside, the small temple of Mentuhotep II and III of the Eleventh Dynasty, from which Senmut drew the basic design of Deir el-Bahri, gleams whitely too. South of it, to the left from Thebes as one looks across the water, Amonhotep III has become the first of her descendants to follow Hatshepsut's example. He too has constructed his own enormous mortuary temple on the West Bank, its entrance avenue flanked by the two colossal statues of himself which in modern times sit silent, faceless and alone in an empty field beside the road, sole vestiges of the building that once stood there. Not long after will come Seti I with his mortuary temple north of Deir el-Bahri; Ramesses II with his Ramesseum; and Ramesses III with his vast additions to Medinet Habu. But for now, only four temples shine from across the river: distant, mysterious, visited only on rare special occasions by the populace, each guarded by its own coterie of priests whose mission it is to tend for, worship and make happy the dead.

A mile behind them in the Valley of the Kings, hidden back among the stark, forbidding crags, still more hundreds of priests are tending the tombs of the first six pharaohs to be buried there. Not until Tuthmose I was it chosen to be the royal burial ground, in the ultimately futile attempt to escape the grave robbers. Tuthmose II, Tuthmose III, Amonhotep II, Tuthmose IV and Hatshepsut in her hastily sealed tomb, destined to be lost over the centuries but now still tended by a small but faithful priesthood, lie in the Valley.

Others began it, but Ramesses II in characteristic fashion tried to take all the credit: the temple of Luxor, home of the god Amon-Ra's wife and son whom he visited each year during the festival of Opet.

On this particular day there is no particular ceremony in Thebes, which makes it something of a rarity. Life is going along in its customary busy, happy fashion, just as it has without a break, the Ancients like to tell themselves—though they know great periods of trouble have actually gone before—since the days of Menes, and as it will go on, they tell themselves, without a break into the limitless, endless future. It is a pleasant, sunny—when is it not sunny?—happy day, filled with the hum of many voices, much commerce, the lowing of cattle, the groans of camels, the baaing of sheep, the neighing of horses and braying of donkeys mingling with the cheerful clamor of the people of the capital of the Two Lands as they go about their daily business.

All is comfortable, all is serene; only in the heart and mind of the gangling youth in the sprawling palace of Malkata across the river does there live the seed which will flower into the near destruction of all this peaceful, ordered life.

No one conceives of such a thing on this particular day, because something truly exciting lies ahead. It is just a week away from Opet, the great New Year Festival that occurs when Amon is taken by water from Karnak to Luxor to visit his wife and son. This occurs annually when Hapi is at full flood, and it lasts for twenty-four days, during which the capital comes to a virtual standstill. Everybody who is anybody comes to Thebes from all over Egypt for the occasion; and right down to the littlest nobody, they all eat too much, drink too much and make love as much as they can. It all begins with great religious solemnity, but as with Hathor's visits to Horus and Edfu, it soon degenerates into one great big glorious happy drunk. Thanks to Amon and praised be his name for furnishing the excuse. Everyone has one whale of a time.

Before this stage is reached, however, Amon gets full due. In the first of the sacred barges launched from Karnak his small gold statue, glittering in the sun, is surrounded by the High Priest and his associates in their formal white robes, chanting their ritual songs and poems to the god. Behind Amon comes the barge of Pharaoh and the royal family, they too chanting faithful obeisance to the god. Then follow lesser priestly dignitaries and high officials of the government. To the shouts and rhythmically clapping hands of hundreds of thousands crowding the Theban waterfront along the two miles between the temples, the procession is towed slowly upstream by many hundreds of lesser priests, slaves and soldiers.

Arrived at Luxor, Amon is borne ashore to the Luxor temple, where there is a pause while acrobats and dancing girls entertain the crowding multitude, many of whom see their pharaoh and the high dignitaries of Amon at such close range on only this one annual occasion. Then bulls, rams and other sacred animals are sacrificed, and offerings are made by the priests to Amon, to his wife Mut and to his son Khonsu, who live in the Luxor temple. Amon is then placed in a chamber beside theirs and the priests begin their twenty-four-day series of rituals, which conclude with the return trip downriver to Karnak, where Amon is returned to his own place in

Ramesses II, ever-ubiquitous, peeks through the shadows as they fall on the Temple of Luxor, conceived and originally constructed by his predecessor, Amonhotep III.

the inner sanctuary amid further offerings, sacrifices and rituals. In the interim, the populace has been on a three-week binge.

History turns full-wheel in many interesting ways. Today there stands like a sore thumb in one corner of the Luxor temple the mosque of Abu el-Hagag, whose Muslim priesthood has successfully defended it for many years against the aesthetically outraged and the archeologically dismayed. Each year during the Muslim ceremony of *Moulid*, sheiks emerge from Abu el-Hagag bearing aloft three small boats which they put on carriages and pull through the city. Streets and buildings are bedecked with flowers. Rhythmic clapping greets the procession. Dancers twirl and stunt along the way. The ceremony does not last twenty-four days, and Muslims being Muslims, it does not descend into the realms of orgy; but the ghost of Opet, like so many other ghosts of Ancient Egypt, lingers on.

The continuity of the Ancients' life, the underlying serenity of it, the smile which seems to have persisted even in the midst of chaos and turmoil, go back to the earliest times and rest upon the firmest of foundations.

It begins with the gods and with things as they were, as the ancient texts put it, "on the first occasion."

On the first occasion there was, as we have noted earlier, the god Atum; and when he appeared in the world it was covered with water, which was known as Nun. Long before the Bible, the Ancient Egyptians conceived of creation rising from a flood. There came a moment when Nun began to recede a little; and on the first hillock to emerge, the first primeval hill—known as the benben—Atum appeared.

This was according to the religion developed where the Rolls-Royces and Mercedes now drive grandly along the streets of wealthy Heliopolis; and since out of the Heliopolitan dogma there came the worship of Ra, and so eventually of Amon-Ra, who came to rule all, it can be said that here truly arose the basic religion of the Ancients. Memphis had the god Ptah, whose children ruled in a golden age and who was worshipped and honored to the end of Ancient Egyptian history. From Hermopolis in Upper Egypt came the idea of a group of eight gods, also including Nun, who ruled together in a golden age. From Thebes came Amon, who eventually was joined with Ra of Heliopolis; and he too founded a golden age.

Golden—always golden. An ideal and idyllic period during which, "on the first occasion," all these gods, of whatever region of the Two Lands, established themselves and ruled for a time in a perfectly planned, perfectly ordered society of which Pharaoh ultimately became the heir, and to whose recapture and preservation Pharaoh and his people were to be dedicated in heart and mind for all their many days.

So Nun receded, as the Heliopolitan story would have it, and there stood Atum, "he who created himself." His principal counterpart in the physical world became the beetle Khe-pe-ru, who pushes a ball of dung, containing, so the Ancients believed, an egg, along the sand before him. (A number of pharaohs, including

Akhetanen—Nefer-Kheperu-Ra—and Tutankhamon—Neb-Kheperu-Ra—had the beetle-god in their throne names.) By the time of the Fifth Dynasty, Atum had become identified with Ra, his emergence from the waters symbolizing the bringing of light to disperse the universal darkness of Nun.

For the time being, however, there he stood, all by himself; and being moved, as were those on earth who later imagined him, by the universal principle of multiplication, he looked about for a mate. There was none and so, as the texts frankly say, he masturbated and produced out of his own seed the Heliopolitan Ennead which in time came to dominate that body of extremely complicated myth which served the Ancient Egyptian for religion. He was regarded in the texts as being bisexual and was sometimes referred to as the "Great He-She." The practical Ancients imagined creation in terms of sexual generation; and Atum, without any false modesty, was believed to be the original creator in the most direct, uncomplicated and no-nonsense fashion.

He spit out his son Shu, vomited forth his daughter Tef-nut. Shu became the life principle, Tefnut his wife. Later she was transmuted—with an ease only the Ancients could muster—into the principle of universal justice and order known as the goddess Ma'at.

First, however, Shu and Tefnut had children, Geb the earth and Nut the sky. Geb and Nut in turn produced Isis and Osiris and Nephthys and Set. The last was the one who created all the trouble, first with his brother Osiris and then with his nephew Horus.

Meanwhile, overjoyed at seeing Shu and Tefnut appear, Atum wept tears which became men. These gave the Ennead something to rule over, and this they did, establishing (aside from their family quarrels) universal peace and order. As creator of mankind as well as the earliest gods, Atum was known as Lord of the Two Lands. Pharaoh inherited this title in due course.

Elsewhere, in Memphis, Ptah was presiding over the same kind of world, in his case with the addition of Thoth, god of wisdom, to help him, and also with some concept of universal good and general moral principle which seems to have been absent—or at least unmentioned in discovered texts—from Atum in his earliest days. And in Thebes, Amon, an invisible force, secret and all-powerful, also was alone, also masturbated, also created other gods, also ruled a world of harmonious order.

Somehow out of these varying dogmas, each with its emphasis on serenity and order, there emerged a whole set of other gods, many springing up individually in the different villages and tiny city-states before the whole became merged into a single kingdom by Menes. When it did, none of the gods was abolished: all were simply absorbed into one great hodgepodge from which the Ancient Egyptian apparently drew at will whichever suited his particular purpose, need and bent of mind.

The great gods of the original time continued to be worshipped through priesthoods of varying degrees of strength, wealth and influence, with Ra and then the combined Amon-Ra eventually emerging as supreme with the rise of the Theban dynasties. Why so many of the gods were given the heads and attributes of birds and animals is unknown, nor is it exactly clear how Pharaoh came to be "the Living Horus," who became transformed into Horus' father Osiris upon his death. Nor do we know exactly how Anubis became appointed to be the guardian of the gate of the afterworld, or Thoth the god of wisdom, or Sekh-met the goddess of war, or Hathor the goddess of well-being and good things. Or why the hippopotamus was worshipped, or Nek-he-bet the vulture or Buto the cobra or Bast the cat. Nor do we know, really, which of these were favored by the ordinary citizen in his private worship, or whether he even paid much attention to them, except as they were backed by vigorous and greedy priesthoods.

The story of Egyptian worship, as with so many things that have come down to us, is largely the story of pharaonic worship, because it was through the pharaohs and at their order that the temples and other depictions of religion came to be. We know which gods mattered most to them, but of the religious inclinations of their humbler countrymen, we know virtually nothing. It is a charming picture to think of the average Egyptian bowing in worship as the spirit moved him, to the passing jackal or the hovering bird, and quite possibly he did. But he surely was no more adept at keeping all the gods and goddesses straight (Ramesses II called on one thousand to witness his treaty with the Hittites) than the rest of us. He knew the major figures, as we do; and that was probably about all he could remember, offhand. And he may well have had household deities of whom Pharaoh in his palace never dreamed; just as Akhenaten was to have his Aten ignored by most of his countrymen.

In the story of the great gods, however, there is illustrated again the essential earthy humanity of these little people, who could conceive of the creator standing on a mound in the middle of an endless ocean, masturbating to begin the world. No such relaxed concept ever found its way into any other religion—certainly not into any major religions of the West. Which accounts, perhaps, for a certain uptightness about a lot of things.

At any rate, in this Thebes of the Eighteenth Dynasty into which we have wandered for a moment, it is of course Amon who rules supreme and Amon who will shortly be worshipped in the festival of Opet. In the meantime, life proceeds in a fashion that bespeaks a common humanity across the millennial gap.

Away from the busy commerce of the river, in quiet places farther from the city, some men are fishing, others are hauling on the *shaduf* or driving an ox in a circle to work the waterwheel, both means of drawing water from the Nile as ancient—and as contemporary—as Egypt itself. Women and children are washing clothing on the stones. Most of the land is inundated at the moment, but in the higher ground men are guiding wooden plows behind oxen or water buffalo, preparing the land for the sowing of grains and vegetables that will follow Hapi's gradual withdrawal over the next month or so. It is a time of repairing and making ready, not only for Opet but for the annual renewal of the land that will follow the inundation.

The shaduf, used to bring the waters of Hapi to the land. Its ancestry goes back further than the pharaohs'.

Elsewhere in their mud huts and hovels, the peasant women are sewing, drying fruit, making pottery, tending the younger children. Some of their houses have two or three rooms, accommodating as many as three generations; others are mere shacks or lean-tos designed to provide minimum protection against the fierce rays of Ra in summer, the cool, sharp winds that blow off the Red Land in winter. Life is simple, hard, filled with the common, necessary tasks of staying alive. It has changed very little, in five thousand years.

There is, of course, an upper class; and, as in Egypt today, the drop from rich to poor is very precipitous and a long way down. If Thebes can be said to have a middle class, it is composed of about the same elements as it is now: scribes, teachers, government workers, higher ranks of the army, the more prosperous and thrifty merchants, those few farmers who have managed to accumulate more than the minimal plot of ground needed for sheer existence. The middle class is not very large and not very wealthy; and while its size and status improves in times of relative peace and prosperity, as it is doing to some modest degree now, it can hardly be said to bridge the enormous gap between the two extremes of society.

But in this society of 3,200 years ago, as in the two millennia preceding it and the one that will follow, there is almost no protest or rebellion against this. The gods in some mysterious fashion seem to have ordained the ranks of society as well as its form; and Pharaoh and his government, as inheritors of the gods, are determined that it shall always be so. Yet there is a surprising scope for talent, even so. Intelligent pharaohs, and many of them were very intelligent, could perceive without difficulty the advantage to them in encouraging bright young men to advance in their service. Many of the most famous nonroyal figures of Egyptian history, men such as Hatshepsut's Senmut, Zoser's Imhotep, Amonhotep III's Amonhotep, Son of Hapu, and the like, were commoners or lesser nobility, some from extremely humble beginnings, some even slaves, who rose through sheer ability to "sit at the right hand of Pharaoh," as so many of them boasted. Society was rigidly stratified, yet constantly, in nearly all reigns, there is the phenomenon of brilliant young men shooting up through the strata to achieve positions of highest importance in the state. It is, once again, one of the many pleasant and admirable inconsistencies of this easygoing, shrewd and likable people.

Although their society was underpinned by a belief in and a longing for what happened "on the first occasion" there seems to have been no body of direct moral principle by which they lived. Indirect, yes: but the stern admonitions of a Jehovah, the "thou shalts" and "thou shalt nots," were not codified in such fashion. Rather, with the rare exception of a pharaoh's admonition to his vizier on the conduct of his office, or some such direct prescription of behavior for a particular situation or public duty, the moral principles of the society were all expressed, in typical fashion, in a mild and indirect way.

The dead noble boasted on his tomb about the good things he had or had not done—"I have given food and shelter to the helpless, I have not hurt any man," and the like—but he only rarely added, "Go thou and do likewise."

It was enough that he had furnished the example, and that in return for it he had been rewarded, as he was also careful to note, by many sons, good crops, good wine and hunting, the favor of Pharaoh. It was clear enough that anyone who wanted to reap the same benefits should follow the same course. No one now can say with certainty that the given lord did follow that course—with a flowery exaggeration typical of expression as one moves on east from the Gates of Hercules, people sometimes claimed (and still claim) to have done a good deal more than they did do. But the example and the precepts were there. Again, however, not stated in an admonitory fashion: just there, in case anyone wished to honor the example.

It was a moral code distinguished by the constant reiteration of the words, "I have not." When the deceased appeared before the forty-two fearsome judges of the afterworld he made what is known as "The Negative Confession" of *The Book of the Dead*—or, more accurately, *The Book of Coming Forth by Day*. He asserted, in part:

"I have not done evil against people. I have not caused misery to my associates. . .I have not known evil and worthless men. . .I have not done evil things. . .

"I have not deprived a humble man of his property . . . I have not inflicted pain. I have not made anyone hungry. I have not made anyone weep.

"I have not committed murder. . .I have not caused anyone to suffer. . .I have not stolen. I have not plundered. . .I have not cursed. . .

"I have not copulated with men . . . I have not been deceitful . . . I have not gossiped. I have not slandered. . .

"I have not copulated with the wife of another man . . . I have not stirred up strife. . .I have not wronged, I have not done evil. . .

"I am pure of mouth and pure of hands. I am one to whom those who see him say: 'Come in peace! Come in peace!'. . .

"I am pure! I am pure! I am pure! I am pure!"

If there seems a certain amount of protesting too much about all this, and if in the course of human nature it seems a little unlikely that anyone, be he saint or demigod, could ever be quite *that* pure, it was a convention that nonetheless gives negative but emphatic support to the picture of a society in which men and women generally tried to get along well and decently with one another. It is the creed of a people who, in the main and allowing for those periods of civil chaos that marred their otherwise well-ordered journey through history, were essentially gentle, unwarlike, tolerant and well-meaning. Lamentations from the First and Second Intermediate Periods, deploring the lawless and murderous state of society, and harsh pharaonic laws such as those promulgated by Horemheb to clear the chaos left by Akhenaten, were the exception rather than the rule. One was expected to do the best one could, and then claim a bit more; and the forty-two judges, while outwardly fearsome, were apparently softies at heart, for there is no record of anyone ever having been denied entrance to the afterworld after reciting his dutiful litany of "I have nots."

On this day in Thebes, while all is in preparation for Opet, one of those who has embarked upon the litany is the Lord Nakht-Sen-Ret, whose sumptuous villa stands out a bit from the center of the city in its own spacious gardens surrounded by a high, protecting wall. Nakhtsenret has been a principal aide to the Vizier of the South, his major charge being to supervise the provisioning of the forts and guard posts that stretch to the Fourth Cataract. He has done this job reasonably well, taking only the usual amount of customary baksheesh on the side from all the various contractors and suppliers with whom he has dealt, and on the walls of his elaborate tomb across the river in the Valley of the Nobles, just south of the Valley of the Kings, he has already had inscribed his negative confession for the forty-two judges to read. Now he has died after a peculiar wasting disease that not all his doctor's chants, magic spells and appeals to the gods have been able to stop. Like Pharaoh and all other Egyptians in these later days, he has upon his death become Osiris. Once this prerogative was reserved exclusively for Pharaoh (as "the Living Horus," Osiris' son, who became Osiris on his death), but over many centuries it has gradually been claimed by everyone. Like all newly created Osirises, Nakhtsenret now briefly lies in state while around him the women of his household throw dust upon their hair, grovel on the ground, and shriek their grief to Ra.

It is not a moment, perhaps, for the visitor to stop and take stock of the house Nakhtsenret lived in; yet since everyone, including his shrieking wife and daughters, knows that he is now on his way to the wonderful and happy afterworld, and that there is no doubt whatsoever that he will survive the forty-two judges' scrutiny and get there, a survey of the premises is not, perhaps, too rude and obvious. Certainly the surroundings are far more sumptuous (though constructed basically of the same mud brick) than those of several other minor Osirises who lie at this same moment in their mud huts in the outlying villages. Their women too are rolling on the ground, covering themselves with dust and wailing, before the bodies are transported, with none of the pomp and ceremony that will attend Nakhtsenret's, to the edge of the desert to be interred in hastily dug graves in the ever-shifting sand.

Nakhtsenret, as befits the station in life to which he rose (in his case not entirely by merit, since his father also had been high in the office of the Vizier of the South, and the hereditary principle in public office is also a feature of Eighteenth Dynasty life), occupied a villa containing some twenty rooms in a suburb, just south of Thebes, which is to Thebes what Heliopolis millennia later will be to Cairo. He was a wealthy man living among wealthy men, and their houses show it. They are all built with a certain similarity as befits the needs of a climate that for most of the year is hot and dry. The lines are square, straight and unadorned, the hallways wide, the windows high and small. From the outside the villa looks something like a fortress, an impression strengthened by the surrounding wall. It is the gardens with their fountains, the rugs on the floors and the friezes on the walls, the furniture made from cedars of Lebanon, the elaborately carved wooden columns of the same material that support the low ceilings, the occasional touch of gold among the pots and dishes and the jewelry of the women, that soften the impression and indicate the status of the occupants.

Basically, Nakhtsenret's home is similar to that of most of his neighbors, and indeed to most of the wealthier private dwellings that have gone before and will come after. Aside from the very rare breaking of the mold, such as the architects of Mentuhotep II and III and Hatshepsut achieved at Deir el-Bahri, neither royal nor private architecture in Egypt changed very much in three thousand years. Why should it? It worked fine as it was. Why disturb a way of building that had always been and would always be—and, essentially, still is? The Ancients were too practical for that.

The basic plan of Nakhtsenret's home is extremely simple. An entry ramp or staircase rising perhaps five feet above ground level to the brick floor of the house, supported by brick columns fortified here and there by stone or wooden pillars, which is supposed to protect the dwelling from the inundation. A wide entry hallway decorated with wooden pillars, going straight back to a large, square, combined living-dining room, its ceiling higher than the rest of the house to permit high, narrow, ventilating windows. The family's private rooms on either side beyond, reached by narrow hallways that bypass the living room. Larders and servants' quarters. A separate cookhouse. An altar in the garden for Nakhtsenret's favorite god, who happens to be Khonsu the moon-god, son of Amon, though for political and career reasons a statue of Amon is dutifully placed beside his son and carefully honored with daily sacrifices.

Also separate from the house are several huts where the servants live, and, at the back, a vegetable garden. A staircase at the back of the main building leads to the roof of the living room, which is used for relaxing during cooler days, and for sleeping on suffocating nights in the dead of summer. Domestic animals, two or three dogs and a few cats, sleep in the yard or pass freely in and out of the house. A simple but effective system of sluices and conduits carries toilet wastes from the bathroom—which, as in modern Egypt, features some form of a seat in a home as well-to-do as Nakhtsenret's, but in the great majority of his countrymen's dwellings is distinguished only by a hole in the floor which is used when the outdoors for some reason is not immediately available.

It is not courtesy to linger too long today in Nakhtsenret's home—his heir, Nakht-Sebek, indicates as much with a questioning glance from red-rimmed eyes. So we move on. But we know that tomorrow Nakhtsenret's body will be placed in the hands of the workers in the "house of purification" and that after the seventy-day process of mummification a final procession will take him across the river to the West Bank and his eternal resting-place.

115

Emerging from the hushed house into the sunlight of Thebes, we move back to the center of the city and once again we hear the clamor of voices, the barking of dogs, the crying of children, the donkeys' complaint, the bustling, hurrying sounds of the marketplace. A jungle of bells, a clop of hooves, the sound of a carriage stopping, and a soft voice says insistently, "Karnak Temple, sir? Ride around city? Luxor Museum? Make you good price, sir?"

We are back in Luxor, a little changed, but not much, from what it was 3,200 years ago.

And now it is time to cross the river, as so many hundreds of thousands from Pharaoh to peasant to camera-toting tourist, have done for so many, many centuries. It is best to get to this early. Except for the rare chilly day in December, January, February, it is usually blazing hot by 10 A.M. It is wise to be back at the hotel by noon, unless one wishes to go later in the day when the tombs and valleys are virtually deserted. This is physically harder but rewarding if one wishes to be alone with what the necropolis offers. There is much to be alone with, and there are times to do it. Probably the first visit is not the time, because it is then that one becomes familiar with the general plan of the necropolis, enters the major tombs and decides what is worth concentrating upon later.

The attractions of the necropolis lie in a great scattered arc that starts roughly a mile west from the Nile and ranges back into the forbidding hills perhaps another mile. Its westernmost limit is the Valley of the Kings; its innermost, the mortuary temple of Seti I, farthest north of all the monuments.

Many of the area's approximately four hundred tombs lie bunched west of Seti's temple. Most were those of court officials and dignitaries of sufficient stature and sufficient favor with Pharaoh to achieve burial on the West Bank. South of them and farther back against the barren cliffs lie Deir el-Bahri and the remains of the Mentuhotep temples. Roughly in front of these, back a bit toward the river, lies the Valley of the Nobles, whose tombs are surrounded by the mud houses of the villagers of el-Qurna, they who still busily and secretly to this day pursue their search for treasures. South of the Valley of the Nobles and again east a bit toward the river lie Ramesses II's Ramesseum with its giant fallen statue, and Amonhotep III's two faceless and forlorn "Colossi of Memnon." Southwest again comes the walled city of the ancient workers, many more tombs of nobles and dignitaries. Back of them toward the west is the Valley of the Queens. Again south and tö the east is Medinet Habu. Finally, farther south, rarely visited save by the tourist with some special interest in the time of Akhenaten, lies the hilly, shard-filled plain that three millennia ago echoed to the laughter and games of four foredoomed children, Akhenaten, Nefertiti, Smenkhara, and Tutankhamon, in these days when it was the site of Amonhotep III's palace of Malkata.

These are the attractions of the necropolis. Above them broods the "Peak of the West," approximately a thousand feet above the valley floor, highest point of the range as one looks across from Luxor. It is the home of the goddess Mertseger, "Mistress of the West"—in other words, queen of the kingdom of the dead. Her name translates roughly as "Beloved of him who makes silence"—Osiris, king of the dead. She was considered to be "the lion of the Peak" who punished sin with illness and death, and at the same time was a kindly deity to the good, protecting them particularly from serpents. With the peculiar consistency typical of the Ancients, she was accordingly represented either as a cobra or as a woman with a cobra's head, the cobra also forming the *uraeus*, fiercely protective as it rears from Pharaoh's crown above his forehead.

An old and creaky motor launch provides the visitor's principal means of crossing the river now. It travels virtually alone where once pharaonic barges and the busy commerce of Thebes commanded every inch of navigable space. It rattles and wheezes across, filled with the sounds of many languages. On the western shore taxi drivers and instant-antique vendors await the new day's prey: all is ready for those who come to do homage in the necropolis. The launch touches shore, is eased against the dock with many shouts and encouragements from the swarming onlookers. The visitors descend and the hubbub begins.

Here as perhaps nowhere else in Egypt the hawkers are in their glory. The government has tried to restrain them a little, and the professional guides aid this with half-hearted attempts at shooing away. But the effort is generally futile, because most of the tourists, after all, want to look. There may just possibly be that real find, somewhere: it is always worth a glance. The trouble is that a glance leads to a shouted offer by the vendor, hands on arms, pushing about, frantic clutchings as white-robed figures circle and swoop, each trying to outdo the other with "genuine" scarabs, "genuine" rings, "genuine" *ushabtis*, "genuine" everything. Some few, more practical and more candid, maintain fixed stalls at the dock or in the Valley of the Kings, their wares frankly displayed for what they are, reproductions, some of them excellent, to be taken home by the average souvenir-hunter with no nonsense about authenticity. But out among the tombs, from old cigar boxes and out from under dirty gelabayas, come treasures presented with a stealthy craft and a fearful looking-about for authority that would do credit to the greatest actors in Egypt. Indeed, these *are* the greatest actors in Egypt. An emphatic tone, repeated rejections and a firm manner usually provide the only means of terminating the performances. Some of them, though, are truly worth the price of admission.

Once ashore and through the swarm, the average visitor is apt to get the lick-and-a-promise treatment. This is not the fault of the guides, most of whom genuinely like their ancient forebears and the chance to tell the foreigner about them. It is rather the fault of the average Egyptian tour, which far too often is a three- or four-day hustle in which the client is expected to see and absorb three thousand years reaching from Abu Simbel all the way downriver to Giza. Seti I's tomb is spectacular ("What a lot of steps!"), Tut's tomb is tiny ("Imagine all that stuff in that little space!"), Nakht's tomb is charming ("Aren't those dancing girls beautiful?"). Names, dates, faces, monuments speed by in a blur broken only by Egyptian beer, lemonade, tea, coffee or Coke at the government restaurant a hundred yards across the sand from the mouth of Tut's tomb. Then back to the landing dock ("Madam! what your last price for this scarab, madam? Your last price, sir, on this figure god Thoth from Eighteenth Dynasty? Genuine, sir, genuine! What your last price? *Last price*, sir?"). Then comes the creaky launch, the hotel at Luxor, the air-conditioned lobby, the sigh of relief, the collapse, the drink: and so much for the Theban necropolis and the kingdom of the dead.

Where pharaonic barges once crossed the Nile from east bank to west, the creaking motor launch now carries the eager tourist bound for the Valley of the Kings.

Above the village of el-Qurna rises
"the Peak of the West,"
home of the forbidding goddess
Mertseger who presides over the
Theban necropolis. At her feet lie
more than four hundred
jumbled tombs of pharaohs, queens,
nobles and the highest officials of
Ancient Egypt.

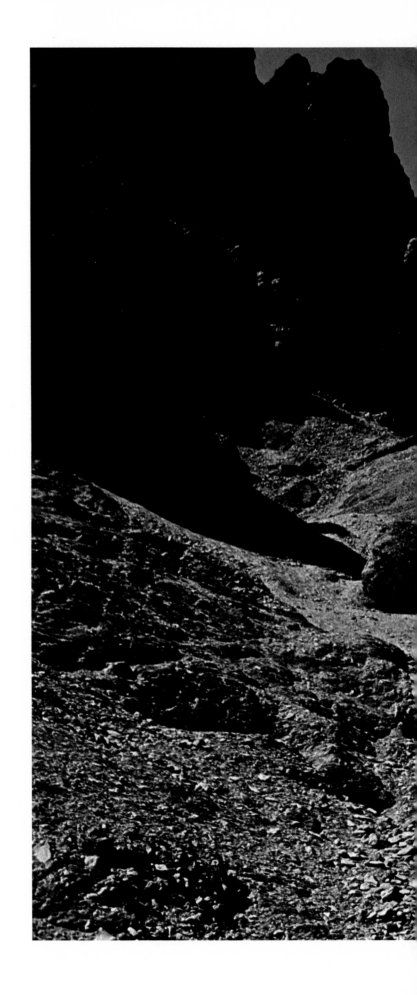

Silence, solitude, desolation—no grimmer or more lonely place could be found than the site the pharaohs chose for their final resting-places in the Valley of the Kings.

There are, however, other ways to do it. One is extremely early in the morning; some guides take their groups across as early as 5 A.M., when all is cool, hushed and quiet. Other individuals who feel hardy enough to do it cross in the afternoon when the necropolis, though blazing with heat, is equally deserted. This is perhaps the better time, as very few more will be coming. The kingdom of the dead lies open. Life slows to siesta above. In the cool tombs below, it continues to move with all the vigor of the high springtime of the ancient world.

In that springtime, pharaohs, queens and nobles alike began the preparation of their tombs long before there was reasonable expectation of death—not because they worshipped death or were obsessed by it or looked forward to it, but simply because they wanted to be sure that when it came they would be suitably housed and that all would be ready for them to enter upon that pleasant aftermath of life that was known as "the Field of Rushes" and "the Field of Offerings." In the Two Fields, which to them were comparable to the Two Lands, they expected to enjoy all the pleasant things they had known on earth.

For the common Osiris in the villages, as we have seen, the expectations of a pleasant afterlife were equally vivid, though the means of securing them infinitely less. In noble and royal household, the means were at hand. In painted scene and priceless artifact, the owners of the tombs thought their future life of comfort was guaranteed; and even though from earliest times the grave robbers industriously removed every priceless thing they could lay their hands on, it is nice to think that in the Field of Offerings and the Field of Rushes the dead of the necropolis are just as happy with their imagined luxuries as though they had never been lost to them—and to us, who would have marveled even more than we do at Tutankhamon's had they been spared.

So for years, in most cases, the work went on. The nearly bare walls and hasty jumble of Tut's tomb are only further proofs that he was, as a sizable school of students believes, hastily murdered and hastily interred. Others, such as the long-lived Seti I and his son, the even longer-lived Ramesses II, had decades in which to have their final resting-places made ready. Tut's relics give an idea, on a relatively modest scale, of what wealth must have adorned his great predecessors' and successors' tombs. But in the paintings there still remains most of what we know—and most of what we need to know—to tell us how the Ancients lived and what their world, in human essentials not so very different from ours or any other, was like.

Before they were able to enter upon their enjoyment of the afterworld which they sought so earnestly to make a counterpart of this, however, they had to survive, be they Pharaoh or commoner, the judgment of the Gods. As noted earlier, there is no record that anyone ever failed to, but the ritual they imagined for themselves was rigorous indeed. From Seti to Ramesses to Hatshepsut to Nakhtsenret to the humblest villager, they all believed—or amiably accepted the myth, we do not know which—that they must go through a lengthy, arduous and highly risky process. In the case of the upper classes this presumably began after the process of mummification; in the case of a deceased too poor for this, he or she must have faced the ordeal at once. But according to the tomb paintings, they all felt it was inevitable. As with so many things, it was a duplicate of what was believed to have occurred "on the first occasion."

If the deceased were wealthy or important enough, the process began with the practice which, second only to the pyramids at Giza, symbolizes Ancient Egypt in the modern mind—mummification. On the instant of death the deceased became one with Osiris and was so referred to: "Osiris Tutankhamon," "Osiris Nakhtsenret," and the like. At the hands of professionals in "the house of gold," or "the place of purification," or "the house of the dead," as it was known in various times and places in the Two Lands, the seventy-day process of embalmment went forward. Wide-eyed Herodotus described it, and his account appears to be generally accurate.

The heart, since it was regarded as the seat of intelligence, was left in the body; all else was removed. An incision in the left side facilitated extraction of stomach, intestines, liver and lungs, which were placed in four jars, later called canopic, bearing the heads of the four sons of Horus. In earlier centuries the body cavity was filled with oils and resins, but from the Middle Kingdom balls of linen were usually used. The brain was also removed through the nostrils, the cavity filled with linen or mud. The body was then left in a bath or packing of natron, a type of salt, until thoroughly dried. A large scarab, sometimes as much as three inches long, was then placed over the heart and the body was swathed in many layers of linen bandages and placed in its coffin. In the case of royalty and nobility there were sometimes as many as three sarcophagi, each slightly larger than the one before, enclosing the coffin. As on "the first occasion," the embalmers took the roles of the gods who assisted Isis when she embalmed Horus. Female relatives, or more usually priestesses hired for the occasion, acted the parts of Isis and Nephthys and kept vigil over the body during preparation.

If the deceased was of sufficient rank to warrant it—and few who were not had such elaborate mummification rites—he or she was then taken by boat across the Nile to the necropolis, with rituals simulating the funeral processions of the pharaohs which went first to the Osiris cult center at Abydos to pay the god final respects before being brought back for interment. The body was then put in place, the ceremony of "the opening of the mouth" was performed by touching the lips with an adze so that they might be opened and the dead might eat and speak in the after-world. The tomb was then closed and the final phase of the deceased's journey to his ultimate happy reward was under way.

It was not, according to the legend painted in the tombs, an easy passage, however certain its outcome may have been. The forty-two judges were waiting and had to be appeased.

After them came an occasion even more impressive: the weighing of the heart. In a great scale in the center of the room Anubis placed in one pan the heart of the deceased, in the other the ostrich feather of the goddess Ma'at, symbol of truth.

Thoth assisted to make sure everything was on the up and up. If the heart and feather balanced one another, the heart was considered truly pure. Thoth wrote this on a tablet, it was shown to the "Great Ennead" of the children of Osiris, and they declared that the deceased need not be thrown to Am-mur, "the Devourer," a grotesque hybrid, part crocodile, part lion, part hippo, who stood nearby waiting to eat the hearts of the guilty.

The deceased then appeared before Osiris, who welcomed him aboard and wished him enjoyment of the Two Fields, reminding him only that, since this was just like home, he would be expected to do his share in cultivating the domains of Osiris and keeping the dikes and irrigation canals in good order. The deceased nodded gravely, knowing full well that his tomb had been filled with several hundred *ushabtis* or "answerers" (for him), the little clay or faience figures who would perform all his duties in his stead. He then walked out a free spirit and went off to fish or hunt or sit and drink beer and wine with his cronies who had gone before, just as always. And out in the heavenly villages along the heavenly Nile, the poorer Osirises were equally at peace, for each of them, however humble his burial place, had a few *ushabtis* to work for him too. And so everybody was happy.

Thus the "death cult" of the Ancient Egyptians: a curiously carefree, light-hearted and happy concept that did a great deal to help keep the society stable. If a man's lot led him to a life spent in village instead of villa, he could always be certain that he could relax in the afterworld; and if life in a villa had its problems for those who were born into it or achieved it, then all would be well later on. The life of the Nile Valley, for all its periods of disruption, some quite terrible, was generally good in the eyes of those whose national memory embraced millennia. Therefore it was only right that it should be preserved. Hence the determination to make sure, misinterpreted for so many centuries by so many people as being simply a gloomy preoccupation with death. On the contrary. It was a happy preoccupation with making sure everything stayed as it was—or as it could be, ideally, if all went well.

For some, of course, particularly those who wore the Double Crown, it was not always that ideal. Even the most successful paid a price; the most famous of all, perhaps, the greatest.

It is very still, very hot; very high above on this lifeless afternoon the goddess Nekhebet the vulture, goddess of Upper Egypt, swings lazily against a dull and leaden sky, her eyes searching ceaselessly for signs of life—or death. Apparently there are none at the moment that appeal to her, for presently she turns on the gentle currents of the upper air, which do not touch us here among the jumble of crags below, and glides away out of sight over the Peak of the West. Perhaps she and Mertseger exchange greetings as she goes; perhaps Mertseger advises her to return before too long. Some small animal, a scorpion, a lizard, Kheperu the beetle, her fellow goddess Buto the cobra, far from her own domain of Lower Egypt, may perish at any time and lie waiting for Nekhebet in the rocks and gorges. Death lives here; and one unhappy youth remains, of all the royal predecessors and successors who were originally buried in the valley, to attest it.

He was eighteen, Neb-Kheperu-Ra Tutankhamon, Lord of the Two Lands, King of the North and South, Mighty Bull, Son of the Sun, Pleasing to Amon (and to Aten, too, before they made him change his name), when they buried him hastily in the smallest kingly tomb in the valley. Now he is a great pharaoh, beloved not only of the Two Lands but of many lands far from the Nile that he could never imagine, but over which his presence has presided in these recent years with all the grace and dignity due it. It is a happy thing for him, though he will never know it—or does he? one is not always so sure of things, when one walks the land of Egypt—and gratifying, that he should receive such tribute. For his was a lonely and beleaguered life, and for once, in his case, the eternal smile is not present. He is represented several times on his sarcophagi and in his funerary effects, and each time his expression grows older, more serious, more troubled. The boy who came to the throne at nine only to die at eighteen from a wound behind his left ear knew few happy days in his brief life. Perhaps those who were responsible for his death could not quite bring themselves to have him portrayed smiling. The thousands who have worshipped him in foreign lands these recent years know little of his tragic story. "Possibly murdered" is as far as it goes. There was more to it than that.

He was, to begin with, son of Amonhotep III, which made him brother to Smenkhara and to the brother he succeeded, "the Heretic," Akhenaten. It was a time of great trouble for the Two Lands, precipitated by the older brother he grew up adoring but was then told he must hate, when he came to the throne. Angry forces raged about the Double Crown. The ins and outs of that unhappy tale belong more to Tell el-Amarna, 250 miles downriver. For now, suffice it to say that Tut was the pawn through whom Amon sought to regain his power, and did.

There are as many guesses as to the family relationships of the closing years of the Eighteenth Dynasty as there are Egyptologists and writers about Egypt. The few scraps of information available to us can be interpreted several different ways. The simplest and most logical is to follow the line of succession, and, fortified by family resemblances, assume that they were exactly what they seemed—that Amonhotep III

Tutankhamon sleeps, at peace at last, while on the walls he is depicted being led through the various passages of the afterworld. Above his head, god Thoth in his form of the baboon enumerates the months, so many of which were unhappy for the beleaguered boy-king.

At a corner of one of Tut's enormous enclosing sarcophagi which now stands in the Cairo Museum, golden goddesses stand guard, charged with protecting his relics through eternity.

was succeeded by his son Amonhotep IV/Akhenaten, which we do know without quibble; that Akhenaten established a co-regency for a short period with his younger brother and lover, Smenkhara; that both were slain in the collapse of the Amarna experiment, to be succeeded by the youngest brother, Tutankhamon; and that after him came the elderly Aye, their uncle and the one thread of continuity through all the Amarna upheaval; and that Horemheb, who referred to himself as the son of Aye, was indeed so, and therefore was not a mysterious and unknown army general from out in left field who suddenly seized the throne, but a cousin of the three brothers who in due course came to power and completed the restoration of Amon that he and Aye had forced the boy Tutankhamon to begin.

If this was the case—and where is there proof that it was not?—then Tut's short life can only have been one of constant worry, constant uncertainty, constant fear and protest from the moment he first realized what was going on around him. His clear-eyed golden portraits indicate him to have been a very intelligent boy; probably by four or five he was aware that deep currents were flowing through the House of Thebes. As Akhenaten moved further and further away from his people, as the Two Lands floundered and foundered under his remote, disinterested rule, there must have been many worried family conferences on what should be done about it. Constantly, too, there must have been pressures upon the family from the underground network of defrocked priests of Amon, humanly anxious to regain their herds, flocks, villages, farms, their enormous wealth and power that had almost equaled Pharaoh's own. Ultimately these came together in a fusion of aims: Akhenaten and Smenkhara must go, the boy Tut, young enough to be dominated and controlled, must be placed upon the throne; the happy childhood that had begun in the palace of Malkata and continued for a time, even in the shadow of troubles, at Nefertiti's palace at Amarna, must come to an end before the stern necessities of state.

And so, one suspects, it came to be. Akhenaten, Smenkhara, Nefertiti, all vanish abruptly from history. Suddenly Tut, aged nine, is on the throne. Horemheb and the priests of Amon must have thought their battle was won. Aye, more equivocal and more devoted to his nephew, could not have been so sure. Events were to bear him out.

All of Tutankhamon's formative years had been passed under the rule of the Aten, Akhenaten's "Sole God," that representation of the solar disk with its long reed-like arms reaching down to give, with tiny hands, blessings to Akhenaten and Nefertiti. Indeed, Tutankhamon's name was not even Tutankhamon at his christening: moved by their own indirect yet obviously determined protest against overweening Amon, Amonhotep III and Queen Tiye had named their third son Tutankh*aten*. Most of his young life had been spent at Akhenaten's new capital of Akhet-Aten, known to us, from the Arabic name conferred many centuries later, as Tell el-Amarna. On many occasions he accompanied his brother and his cousin Nefertiti as they paid worship to their god; everything he saw and lived through up to age nine was conditioned and dominated by Aten. How could he have been other than a

Four "canopic jars," each lidded with the head of one of Horus' four sons, contained the entrails of the dead. Two of Tut's gleam in alabaster purity in the dusky corridors of the Cairo Museum.

devoted Atenist himself, particularly since he was fortified in this by his personal devotion to Akhenaten and Nefertiti?

Suddenly, probably in Amarna, there came a knocking in the night, the admonition by Aye or Horemheb or both that he must rise and come forward, for he now was king. Suddenly the world of the Aten was swept away. Amon was back in power, and Tut, guided and controlled by his uncle and his tenacious cousin, was to be his staff and surety. Aged nine, without army, friends, supporters, adherents, in a palace revolution in which the popular will played no part because there was no will but Pharaoh's—what could he have done but what he did?

It was not done, however, without a clash of wills that persisted through his reign. They wanted him to marry Akhenaten's remaining oldest daughter, Ankh-e-sen-pa-Aten, which would guarantee his succession through the female line. She was a little older, but she was his niece and they had been playmates and companions all their lives: he did not mind that. They forced her to change her name, as they had forced him, to Ankh-e-sen-*Amon*. She resented that as bitterly as he, but they had no choice. Yet all about them they kept the signs and symbols of the Aten, even as the people were told that Amon was back, and even as work went forward on the restoration of his temples and on those of the other gods brought low by Akhenaten. On one of the most spectacular items found in his tomb, their golden throne that stands now in the Cairo Museum, they had themselves portrayed sitting beneath the Aten, whose spidery arms and little hands reach down to confer upon them the same blessings he had given Akhenaten and Nefertiti.

So the time came when it was necessary to remove him too. He was nearing eighteen. Very soon the regency would have to end and he would take over the full powers of Pharaoh. The intelligent eyes that understood so much kept company with a will increasingly determined. The ordered society of the Two Lands, thrown into such chaos by his brother and only now beginning to be put right again by Horemheb, Amon and Aye, could not be disrupted a second time. They who had regained power were determined to keep it.

Once again there was commotion in the night. Somewhere in a long-lost palace in Thebes, to which they had all returned from abandoned Akhet-Aten, or across the river in once-happy Malkata, the blow fell upon the sleeping skull. The intelligent eyes went out forever, and Aye, sickened and saddened but doing his duty by the Two Lands as he always had, became the wearer of the Double Crown.

There was great haste, then. The small tomb among the eerie rocks was opened and crammed full of all the hodgepodge of his reign, and some from Akhenaten's as well. It may not even have been his tomb at all, to begin with; there is some speculation it might have been prepared originally for Smenkhara. Certainly it was small, barren, undecorated save for the burial chamber itself, with its frieze of Thoth as baboon, and Aye, wearing the leopard skin of the High Priest of Amon, presiding over the ceremony of the Opening of the Mouth. But inside, jammed in with furtive and guilty haste, what a treasure lay. "Wonderful things!" exclaimed Howard Carter in hushed, spine-tingled awe in 1922. And wonderful they are, these relics of the youngest of pharaohs who never was allowed the chance to fulfill the promise of the clear, intelligent eyes and the level, steady glance.

Perhaps it was better for the Two Lands that it should be so. Perhaps he would have tried to restore the Aten, as there is evidence he was determined to do. Perhaps things would no longer have been as they were "on the first occasion." Perhaps, for he looks to be much less the fanatic and much more the careful mind than his brother, his revolution would have transformed the country far beyond Akhenaten's; and the long tale might have ended far, far sooner, and in a much, much different way.

He rests there now, the only pharaoh who still lies in the Valley of the Kings. The others, such as have been recovered, and many have, lie side by side in the long, glass-cased windrows of the Mummy Room of the Cairo Museum. It is sad that they are not here; it is fitting that he is. Nekhebet sails slowly over, Mertseger guards him from the Peak. The tourists in their endless thousands come to pay tribute, as they have to his relics in so many lands.

He was very young, Neb-Kheperu-Ra, and only a promise of what he might have been. But to him, as to Hatshepsut before him, time and the strangeness of fate have given the final word. His death was his triumph. Three thousand years later it made of him the perfect symbol of the Two Lands whose king he was in a span too brief for deeds but ample enough for glory.

Again, it is hot, very hot; and very still. The last buses and cars, save one, have come and gone. Only two weary but still hopeful vendors remain at the gate, cigar boxes filled with genuine-found-in-temple-sirs discoveries. Ahead the long steps lead up. Somewhere there is a clash of arms, a blare of trumpets, a high, clear, feminine voice commanding silence. The Good God Ma-ke-Ra Hatshepsut, King of the North and South, Lord of the Two Lands, Mighty Bull, darling of Amon and indeed, as she tells you on the walls of this her temple Deir el-Bahri, his daughter, advances. All prostrate themselves and "smell the earth," as the old texts put it. With Senmut at her side she stands for a moment surveying the perfectly proportioned building that rises above, outlined against the desolation of the jagged cliffs that seem almost to be on the verge of toppling forward to obliterate her monument. Then she makes a gesture, and, hand on Senmut's arm, begins the long climb up. It is the day of dedication and she has come across the river from Thebes in all her panoply to do it.

Thus it is easy to imagine her, as one moves slowly up those same steps in the heavy heat 3,300 years later. On her obelisk across at Karnak she instructs the visitor to acknowledge, "How like her it is!" about that accomplishment. The thought intrudes almost everywhere in this most beautiful and most feminine of buildings. She was quite a girl, was Hatshepsut who became Makera, queen who became king, woman who became man for the purpose of her regal divinity. She lost her throne and her life, eventually, to her hated half brother and husband, Tuthmose III; but she reigns in imagination and memory as his equal, still. And, as with Ramesses II after her and many before, there is no false modesty in her accounting of it. She is, if anything, more boastful than they, if it is possible for one pharaoh to outbombast another in the long record of self-praising statements they have left us.

At the beginning of the series of scenes at Deir el-Bahri which relate Hatshepsut's original version, Amon is portrayed telling Thoth (who seems to have been around at most significant moments in most pharaohs' lives), "I will unite for her the Two Lands in peace . . . I will give to her all lands, all countries."

Thoth, that crafty intelligent one who always looks more innocent and saintly in his guise of the ibis than he does as an ape, tells Amon how to go about it. The king (Tuthmose I), he says, is an old man, born of common parentage, whose claim to the throne rests on his marriage to Queen Ahmose of the royal line. Thoth suggests that while the king is away, Amon should visit Ahmose.

Next the two of them are seen together. The text behind Amon relates that "he made his form like the majesty of this husband. He found her as she slept in the beauty of her palace. She waked at the fragrance of the god, which she smelled in the presence of his majesty. He went to her immediately, he cohabited with her, he imposed his desire upon her, he caused that she should see him in his form of a god. When he came before her, she rejoiced at the sight of his beauty, his love passed into her limbs, which the fragrance of the god flooded; all his odors were from Punt."

Ahmose, properly overwhelmed, exclaims, "How great is your fame. It is splendid to see your front; you have united my majesty with your favors, your dew is in all my limbs."

"After this," the inscription adds, "the majesty of this god did all that he desired with her."

And so came Hatshepsut. In swift succession the scenes of her birth and acceptance by the gods and people proceed along the temple walls, until she is able to tell us that "Her Majesty grew beyond everything; to look upon her was more beautiful than anything... her form was like a god, she did everything as a god, her splendor was like a god; Her Majesty was a maiden, beautiful, blooming... She made her divine form to flourish, the gift of him who fashioned her."

It is then related how Tuthmose I summoned the court, presented Hatshepsut and declared that "she is my successor upon my throne, she it assuredly is who shall sit upon my wonderful seat. She shall command the people in every place of the palace; she it is who will lead you; you shall proclaim her word, you shall be united at her command. He who shall do her homage shall live, he who shall speak evil in blasphemy of Her Majesty shall die."

Thereupon everybody rejoices and when her accession is announced to the populace, "they leaped and they danced..."

Surveying all this on the day of dedication, this determined little character, whose statues almost all do display the smile, serene and self-satisfied, must have murmured complacently to herself, "How like me it is!" as she climbed the steps. Because it was, indeed. The divine birth was a handy fiction, the coronation scene as she related it was obviously concocted for political purposes to strengthen her claim against that of Tuthmose III; and all in all, she had a right to be well pleased with herself. She undoubtedly thought: *So much for Brother.*

(Whose agents, as noted, must have been somewhat half-hearted about it when he regained the throne and it came time to hack all this out, because quite enough of it is left to proclaim Hatshepsut's personal version of her story.)

The time came, of course, when Brother did return, with a vengeance; but in the meantime there were the obelisks, the placid journeys up and down the Nile, the peaceable aspects (except for the family feud) of a female reign. And finally there came the expedition to Punt which will always be associated with her name—not because it actually accomplished so very much, but simply because it succeeded in getting safely there and safely back, and because it was the first major attempt by a pharaoh (save an earlier inconclusive one by a Sesostris of the Twelfth Dynasty) to penetrate that mysterious land that intrigued so many of them. A dusty region, not as attractive as Egypt, somewhere down toward what is now Somalia, became in the Egyptian mind a romantic never-never land filled with myrrh and incense. It apparently had them, but not much else of note save a top-heavy queen who rode a donkey a third her size. Nonetheless, throughout Egyptian history Punt remains a

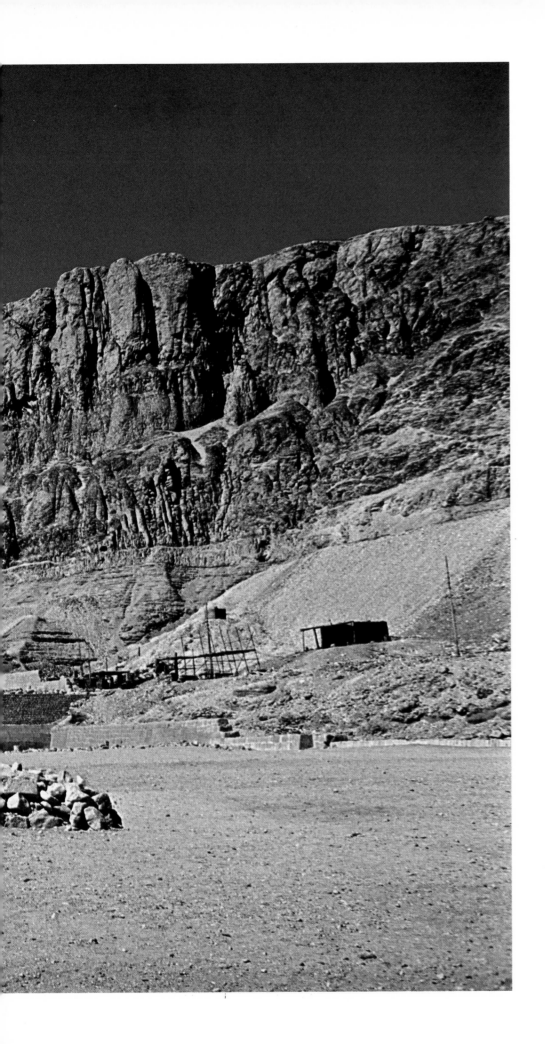

Here she stood 3,400 years ago,
surveying with satisfaction the most
beautiful and artistically pleasing
of all pharaonic temples.
Beneath the forbidding, protective
cliffs the modern visitor views
Hatshepsut's Deir el-Bahri with
much the same delight she must
have felt herself.

romantic and ever-beckoning mirage. Hatshepsut, however, is the only pharaoh who apparently organized and sent forth an expedition which in modern terms might be called "scientific"—with the specific purpose of visiting the place and bringing back whatever unusual items could be found there.

Again, she tells the story in full on the walls of Deir el-Bahri, and this time there is no reason to believe that her account is not basically factual.

Five vessels set sail on the expedition, and since they are shown subsequently both in the Red Sea and on the Nile, the assumption is that a canal connecting the two had been built some time prior to the Eighteenth Dynasty, perhaps during the Twelfth.

They go at the command and with the aid of "the Lord of Gods, Amon, lord of Thebes, presider over Karnak," because, Hatshepsut relates with characteristic modesty, he loved her "more than the other kings who have been in this land forever."

Given such backing for such reason, the expedition could do no other than arrive safely in Punt and come safely home again, and that it is shown doing. Much booty is presented to Hatshepsut.

"Never," she remarks complacently, "was brought the like of this for any king who has been since the beginning." She presents the gifts to Amon and describes herself in the third person with suitable approval:

"She has no enemies among the Southerns, she has no foes among the Northerns; the heavens and every country which the god has created, they all labor before her. They come to her with fearful heart, their chiefs with bowed head, their gifts upon their back. They present to her their children that there may be given to them the breath of life, because of the greatness of her father, Amon, who has set all lands beneath her sandals."

Then she speaks directly:

"I shine forever in your faces through that which my father Amon has desired. . . I will cause it to be said to posterity: 'How beautiful is she, through whom this has happened,' because I have been so very excellent to him, and the heart of my heart has been replete with that which is due to him. I am his splendor on high and in the nether world. I have entered into the qualities of the august god. . . He has recognized my excellence, that I speak a great thing which I set among you. It shall shine for you upon the land of the living. . . that you may grasp my virtues. I am the god, the beginning of being, nothing fails that goes out of my mouth. . . You shall fulfill according to my regulations without transgression of that which my mouth has given. He has desired me as his favorite; I know all that he loves. . ." But, still, came Brother; and presently she vanishes, done to death in some secret way in some secret place, at his command; and the busy chisels go to work to disfigure the tales she told and the proud boasts she made; and Tuthmose III, safe upon the throne at last, sets forth upon his great campaigns of conquest.

Hers was a reign intensely feminine and intensely selfish. Everything she does is done for Amon, everything she wished preserved is addressed to the glory of the god. There is no indication, no slightest selfless hint that in his glory, and in what she did for it, lies glory for Egypt as well. No single thought of Egypt *as Egypt* seems ever to have crossed that ambitious little mind. There is none of that thread of *service to Egypt* that distinguishes many pharaohs great and less great. Even pompous, often laughable Ramesses II—"the Great"—with his bumbling escape from his "victory" at Kadesh and his self-proclaimed "triumph" over the Hittites, was fighting for Egypt and was serving, as he saw it, Egypt's people as well as Egypt's god. In Hatshepsut everything is turned inward upon her diety with a fanaticism almost as intense, if not as disruptive, as Akhenaten's. Tuthmose III fought *for Egypt;* he was protecting her borders, expanding her power, making great her people. He, like many others, had some concept of duty *to Egypt.* Not so his sister.

But she lives on, mocking him still, and while historians know what Tuthmose did—and his own proud boasts proclaim it—he is not called to the attention of visitors to the Two Lands now and it is not to him that they pay their tribute. It is to the Lady of Deir el-Bahri, whose beautiful temple is being beautifully restored, and whose triumphant smile, never troubled, never doubting, shines forth with bland assurance wherever she is met throughout the world, in the museums of Cairo and New York and many points between.

Amon loved her, Hatshepsut said, "more than the other kings who have been in this land forever ... I will cause it to be said to posterity, 'How beautiful is she...'"

It is still hot—but, come, is it rarely anything else?—as one approaches the grandest tomb of all, that of Seti I, just a few yards past the restaurant from Tutankhamon's. How mundane, yet in a sense how human, it is, that the greatest in size and the greatest in fame should be separated by the noisy haven where overheated tourists gulp their beers and lemonades at prices that might make even a pharaoh pause.

Seti I and his son, Ramesses II, whose Ramesseum stands in impressive ruin some two miles south along the necropolis' edge, are linked inseparably in the story of Egypt. The Ramesses we left brooding patiently above Lake Nasser at Abu Simbel far to the south was in many ways, for all his pomposity and sometimes rather ridiculous self-aggrandizement, a remarkable figure; and he was the son of a remarkable father, less publicized because he did not have Ramesses' enormous ego and drive for personal advertisement, but nonetheless one of the hardest working, most conscientious and most effective of all the pharaohs. His mummy in the Cairo Museum looks handsome, stern and indomitable; and so he was.

After Akhenaten came Tutankhamon—Aye—and Horemheb the great restorer, whose thirty-five years, or thereabouts, upon the throne were basically devoted to bringing stability and civil order back to a Two Lands sadly disrupted by the Amarna revolution and its uncertain aftermath under Tut and Aye. Horemheb did not look outward: there was more than enough to attend to at home. He wrought well, however.

Unlike Hatshepsut, his proudest boast, and a true one, was: "Behold, his majesty spent the whole time seeking the welfare of Egypt." When in his seventies he arranged that the succession should pass to his elderly friend and army companion who became Ramesses I, Egypt was stable again.

There had long been growing in the mind of Ramesses I's son, Seti, by then approaching his thirtieth year, the conviction that it was time for Egypt to regain her lost empire. The dream was to consume the energies of himself, his own son, and their successors for many years thereafter.

Ramesses I reigned alone for perhaps one year, during which he began construction of the great hypostyle hall at Karnak, completed by his successors to the bedazzlement of all who see it now. Seti was associated with him as co-regent for perhaps another year, during which there may have been a minor expedition to Nubia; and then Ramesses died, leaving the throne in the hands of the second great conqueror of the Eighteenth Dynasty, who lost no time in getting on with the job.

Very soon after his coronation Seti set out, following almost the exact line of campaign as that of his great military predecessor, Tuthmose III. Through southern Palestine to northern, then on to the Lebanon; and the siege of another Kadesh, this one on the Orontes River, a center of rebellion since the days when Akhenaten dreamed away the empire.

Wearing the leopard skin designating the High Priest of Amon, Seti I stands frozen forever, imperious and stern, on the wall of his tomb.

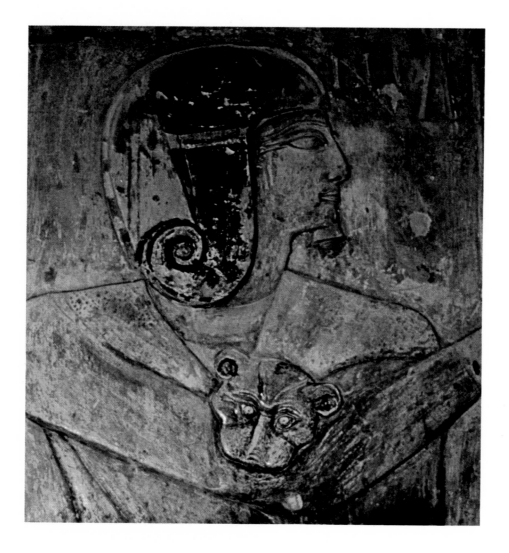

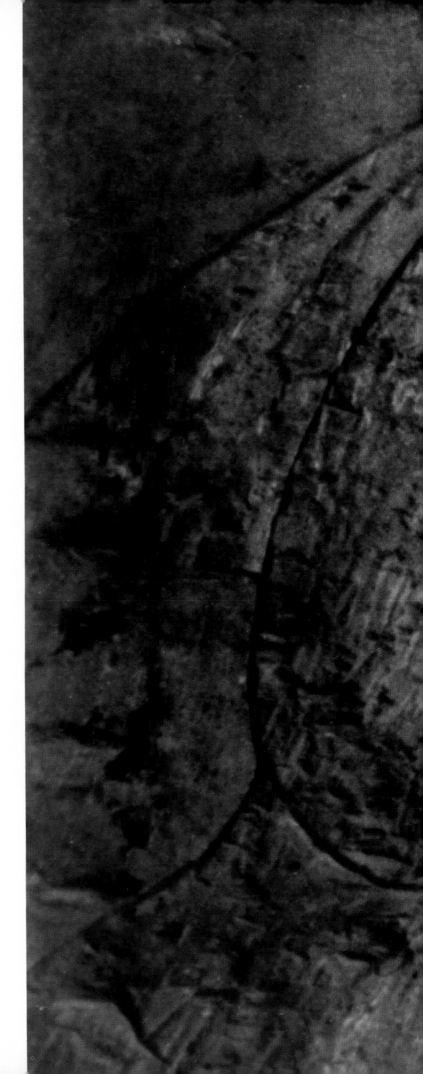

Seti I had built for himself the grandest tomb in the Valley of the Kings, and proudly had it inscribed, "Behold, His Majesty spent the whole time seeking the welfare of Egypt." And so this good man and valiant military leader appears to have done. In his enormous and elaborately decorated mausoleum is exhibited to the full the Ancients' abhorrence of a blank wall: virtually every inch is covered with hieroglyph, painting, or inscription. Among the most impressive is the depiction of the beetle god Kheperu, believed to be the symbol of creation, life and good luck.

In the extensive reliefs that Seti had carved on the north wall of Karnak to commemorate his campaigns, he is referred to, significantly, as "the king who protects Egypt," and so he evidently regarded himself. Much tribute and obeisance is paid to Amon, but the king's own will is given proper place. He is also portrayed, partly for propaganda purposes, as a fairly bloodthirsty individual:

"Lo, as for the Good God, he rejoices to begin battle, he is delighted to enter into it, his heart is satisfied at seeing blood, he cuts off the heads of the rebellious-hearted, he loves an hour of battle more than a day of rejoicing. His Majesty slays them at one time. He leaves not a limb among them, and he that escapes his hand as a living captive is carried off to Egypt."

He is also shown slaying with his own hand in the temple of Karnak the captive rebel chieftains whom he has brought back to Thebes as a sacrifice to Amon. He meant business.

It was good that he did, because no sooner had he triumphed in Palestine and recovered major areas of the north than the Libyans were once more nagging away on the west. His entire second year on the throne was spent in the western Delta driving back these bothersome neighbors. This accomplished, he had to turn northward again to restore Egyptian power in Syria and to engage in the first clash with the rising kingdom of the Hittites. Like his son after him, he soon perceived that to contain the Hittites by force of arms would require constant campaigning, and so he presently signed a treaty with them which apparently held for the rest of his reign. Having thus restored a major portion of the old Empire, he then turned to the restoration of the Eighteenth Dynasty temples devastated by Akhenaten, and in this pursuit passed the rest of his days. He it was who made a modest start on the temple at Abu Simbel. It remained for his egomaniac son to appropriate it, expand it enormously, and divert its purpose to his own aggrandizement rather than to the glory of the gods, whom he tucked away inside in the form of statues much smaller than his.

Seti was a conscientious soul and took a pride completely unknown to Hatshepsut in his treatment of his people.

He records with considerable satisfaction how, traveling in the desert west of Edfu, "He stopped on the way to take counsel with his heart, and said: 'How miserable is a road without water! How shall travelers fare? Surely their throats will be parched. What will slake their thirst? The homeland is far away, the desert wide. Woe to him, a man thirsty in the wilderness! Come now, I will take thought for their welfare and make for them the means of preserving them alive, so that they may bless my name in years to come, and that future generations may boast of me for my energy, inasmuch as I am one compassionate and regardful of travelers."

At Abydos, which can be visited in a day out of Luxor, he began the building of the only other temple in Egypt that matches Deir el-Bahri in beauty, a seven-halled sanctuary dedicated to the six great gods of the Osirian Ennead and to himself,

The walls of Seti's tomb illustrate that universal propensity of the Ancient Egyptians to cover every inch with the signs and symbols of their strange hieroglyphic language.

its carvings and colorings still as delicate today as they were 3,000 years ago. (It is there also that the fortunate visitor in recent years has been able to meet a delightful relic of pharaonic times—one of the last of the great English eccentrics, a lady known as "Um Seti," or "Mother of Seti," which she has actually believed for many years that she is. With a tolerant kindness that says something quite special about the present-day Egyptian people, the government has permitted her to live close to the temple and has made arrangements for her to be buried in its precincts when she dies.)

Abydos is a dream of alabaster, fitting monument for the seat of the Osiris cult and the site of the very ancient tombs of First and Second Dynasty kings which lie behind it. On its walls Seti caused to be chiseled a list of their names, which forms one of the most important clues left to their chronological progression. He also ordered that funerary rites and tributes, abandoned for almost two thousand years, be revived in his temple in their honor. Seti I was, in general, nice to everybody, except the unfortunate chieftains who opposed him in his early days after he set out to restore as much as he could of the Empire. Once that was accomplished, his subject peoples found themselves with an amiable and easygoing conqueror. He is among the most likable of the pharaohs; and it is in his tomb, perhaps more than at Abydos or anywhere else among his extensive constructions, that visitors find themselves most overwhelmed and impressed by Seti and his world.

There is the experience of going down—and down—and down—and down, 475 feet into the depths of the mountain. There is the experience of seeing a tomb in which every wall is covered with scenes of Pharaoh's life, scenes of his journey to the afterworld, scenes of the great gods of the Ennead playing their proper legendary roles in the management of the world. The tomb was robbed unknown centuries ago. None of the treasures placed with Seti's body by his son and the priesthood of Amon remain; but the only defacement of the paintings is the darkening of some sections of the roof by the candle smoke of early Christians who hid there. Otherwise the colors are as fresh, vivid and intricate as the day they were painted, an index to Seti's world and to the great gods, their lives and their legends.

The Ancient Egyptians hated a bare wall, and in Seti's tomb they outdid themselves. Scarcely an inch has escaped its hieroglyph, its scene or its symbol. And all of this, it must be remembered, was not designed for human eyes to see. We are interlopers here. All of this strange and fabulous beauty was sealed away when Pharaoh was buried. All of this infinitely detailed, years-long work was designed for his eyes alone, when he began his life in the afterworld. And so it was with all other pharaonic tombs. They were not intended to entertain the casual visitor; they were designed for a single imperial glance. It is one of those points at which the modern mind and the ancient part company completely. How could so much beauty be created, when the sole intention was to seal it forever from living eyes? One can only marvel: there is no point of contact.

In Seti's tomb the kindly cow-goddess Hathor is attended in appropriate fashion by her worshippers.

As to the early days of the monumental ego who now succeeded Seti I, two of the greatest scholars, James H. Breasted and Sir Alan Gardiner, are in the direct disagreement so typical of professional Egyptologists when confronted by the tantalizing scraps of the past. Breasted believes Ramesses II to have been a minor son who got rid of an elder brother who was legitimate crown prince, and thus intrigued and probably murdered his way to the throne in Seti's dying days. Gardiner accepts Ramesses' own story that he was the legitimate crown prince and served as co-regent with his father, succeeding with all due propriety to the throne.

With all respects to Sir Alan, human nature, and particularly Ramesses' own nature as displayed in his overweening self-aggrandizements from one end of the Two Lands to the other, would seem to give the decisive weight to the Breasted interpretation. Standing in the heat and stillness of the Ramesseum two miles south of Seti's tomb, reflecting on the original of the colossal statue that lies jumbled and broken at its eastern gate, one can find no other logical conclusion.

Ramesses tells a good story, in the enormously lengthy inscription he caused to be placed on the wall at Abydos. But the walls of Karnak, that even greater national archive, do not bear him out.

"The Universal Lord himself [Seti]," he says at Abydos, "magnified me while I was a child until I became ruler. He gave me the land while I was in the egg, the great ones smelling the earth before my face. Then I was installed as eldest son to be hereditary prince upon the throne of Geb [the earth-god] and I supervised the state of the Two Lands as captain of the infantry and the chariotry. When my father appeared in glory before the people, I being a babe in his lap, he said: 'Crown him as king that I may see his beauty while I am alive.' And he called to the chamberlains to fasten the crowns upon my head. 'Give him the Great One [the uraeus] upon his head,' said he concerning me while he was on earth."

It is fascinating to imagine how such statements came about. Did Ramesses sit in his palace some night, sucking on a stylus and writing all this down on a papyrus, editing and re-editing until the fiction was exactly as he wanted it? Or did he say to some trusted scribe, "Here, Sekh-nem, write me up a good first draft and be sure to get in the babe-in-the-lap and the uraeus bit?"

It does not, in any event, ring true. It is not our boy as we now know him. Far more in character is the Breasted interpretation, which, based on insertions and erasures in Seti's account at Karnak of his battle with the Libyans reveals the shadowy figure of a prince—not Ramesses—who was apparently Seti's eldest son and the true crown prince.

The pouting boy who sits to the right, first of the four figures at Abu Simbel, showed his ambitious precocity at an early age. The eldest son, name unknown to history, was the legitimate heir. Ramesses, son of a secondary queen named Tuya, was named after his grandfather Ramesses I and thus early given dreams of future glory. When Seti died Ramesses II, perhaps seventeen or eighteen at the time, did

Seti and a fellow deity contemplate each other and eternity on the wall of the most elaborate tomb in the Valley of the Kings.

not hesitate. He moved at once to organize a coup, had his half brother murdered, and seized the crown.

The figure of the Karnak wall was immediately erased and replaced with Ramesses' own, bearing the title "crown prince." Coming to Thebes at once, he further clinched his hold on the loyalties of Amon by joining in the celebration of Opet and giving lavish donations to the god. If the true crown prince had any supporters, they apparently were eliminated, or changed allegiance, with extreme rapidity. Ramesses was on the throne, and there he was to remain for sixty-seven years. It was about then, one suspects, that he stopped pouting and began to smile.

And, of course, he had a good deal to smile about—the longest confirmed reign of any pharaoh; prodigious progenitor of more than 150 children; completer of his father's work in restoring the Empire; battler against the Hittites, now pressing ever more vigorously upon Egypt's borders; survivor of the battle of Kadesh, in which his personal bravery was apparently great even if his overall common sense and generalship were not.

And builder—how he built! Abu Simbel. The Ramesseum. Completion of the hypostyle hall at Karnak. Extensive additions to Karnak and to the Luxor temple. Completion of Abydos. Obelisks and minor temples beyond the scope of modern discovery to number. Statues to himself that strew the land—again, their full number not even scratched, probably, by modern research. And, until he began at last to slip toward senility as he approached his nineties, one of the most vigorous, active and effective of all the pharaohs—mostly in the creation of his own legend, it is true, but busy. Busy, busy, *busy*. And, as he proudly orders himself to be described, like his father one "whose might defends Egypt . . . whose sword protects the Egyptians . . . defender of the Two Lands."

One of his first official acts was to complete Seti's half-finished temple at Abydos, taking the occasion to have chiseled upon its walls the lengthy statement that not only attempted to nail down the legitimacy of his succession to the throne but also appealed to Seti, who was now among the gods, to intercede with them in his son's favor and ensure him a long and fruitful reign. With its bombastic allegations of virtue and its cheerful mingling of fact and fiction, mostly the latter, it is one of the major examples of the Ancients' conviction that the word was as good as, if not better than, the deed; and that if you said something long enough and loudly enough and emphatically enough, it would be so. In Ramesses' case, it was, for it presumably convinced many people then, and it has certainly convinced a lot since.

By the fourth year of his reign, still in his early twenties, he was prepared to embark upon his dearest ambition, the full reconquest of the empire Akhenaten had allowed to slip away.

He didn't make it; but, typical of the Ancients, he said he did—and he said it—and he said it—and he said it. And presently, in the minds of his people, and of many others over the centuries, he became believed. "The Great" was added to his

The beetle god Kheperu, symbol of life, is everywhere.

name, though his greatness lies more in longevity and a furious show of activity than in any lasting achievement other than the glorification of his own ego in temple, statue and hieroglyphic bombast. But the label sticks and the impression lives. He "conquered" the Hittites by prudently deciding it was time to sign the famous treaty witnessed by the thousand gods of Egypt and the thousand gods of the Hittites. And he "won" the battle of Kadesh that he makes so much of in all his boastings, by bumbling into the middle of it, having the courage and the sheer dumb luck to fight his way out of it alive, and then by announcing blandly forever after that he had carried the day by great courage—which was true, when nothing else was left him—and great generalship, which was not true under any circumstances.

He was a shrewd-enough tactician to realize that Kadesh, which had been the key to the successful conquests of his great predecessor Tuthmose III, should be the key to his too: and so he set forth with four divisions of troops, comprising an army of perhaps twenty thousand, to meet Metella, the Hittite king, who had made of the city his principal fortification.

As he finally neared Kadesh after the long march up from Egypt, Ramesses grew so anxious to join battle that he not only led his own division, named for Amon, far ahead of the other three divisions but he even plunged on ahead of the Amon division itself. This recklessness was based upon the tale told by two Bedouin who had been sent out, unbeknown to our hero, by Metella for the express purpose of telling him that the Hittite troops were widely dispersed and a long distance away. Gullible Ramesses, accompanied by only a handful of his household troops, rushed eagerly on ahead to establish a camp and lounge a bit while his other troops caught up. Meanwhile the Hittite king, using the city as a shield between him and Ramesses to conceal the movement of his troops, quickly moved them into position and proceeded to cut the Egyptians in two.

In wild disarray they fled toward their pharaoh, still dawdling comfortably in his camp. The Hittite chariotry surrounded him. Rising now to the occasion with genuine bravery, he rallied the handful of troops remaining and began a series of charges against the weakest point in the Hittite line, so desperate that they finally halted the Hittite advance. It was further slowed by the Hittite troops' sudden abandonment of pursuit in order to loot the defenseless Egyptian camp.

For three hours or more battle swayed hectically back and forth until finally a fresh division of Egyptian troops, perhaps arriving from the direction of the Phoenician coast, came to Ramesses' rescue. Both sides were exhausted and Ramesses thankfully withdrew and scurried back to Egypt. But that, of course, was not the end of it.

At Abu Simbel, Luxor, Karnak, the Ramesseum, Abydos, and on other buildings since lost, he ordered the story of Kadesh told, told, and retold. He does not claim to have captured it, which some recent accounts have kindly done for him, but he certainly makes a point of what he did in the midst of battle "while he was alone, having no army with him."

The head of Ramesses II has toppled to the ground at the Ramesseum in the Theban necropolis, but his placidly smiling visage would indicate that it doesn't trouble him in the least.

The phrase is repeated everywhere. To his titles on his monuments he added, "Prostrator of the lands and countries while he was alone, having no other with him." It was a heady business for a still very young man, and he never got over it even as an old one; although he was sufficiently bright to realize that his precipitous rout, however distinguished by his personal bravery, had left the prestige and power of Egypt in very sad condition in the north.

For some fifteen years he sought sporadically and unsuccessfully to re-establish his control there; until finally Seti and the gods came to his assistance with one more stroke of unexpected luck. Metella died and his brother Khetasar came to the throne. Probably because he too had his internal problems and was exhausted by the constant fighting, he suggested peace. The famous two-thousand-god treaty was signed. Ramesses, true to form, immediately set carvers to work at Thebes and everywhere else establishing his claims of victory.

Yet a dispassionate examination of the only record of actual battle that we have, Kadesh, shows him to have been a headstrong, courageous and not very bright individual who escaped by the skin of his teeth and really accomplished very little at all.

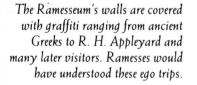

The Ramesseum's walls are covered with graffiti ranging from ancient Greeks to R. H. Appleyard and many later visitors. Ramesses would have understood these ego trips.

But peace, traveler. Look at Abu Simbel! Look at the Ramesseum! Look at the walls of Karnak and the temple of Luxor and the great statue recumbent in the ancient northern capital of Memphis, and the commanding statue standing in Station Square in Cairo, and at all his other statues, monuments and inscriptions scattered throughout Egypt and the world.

The story of Winston Churchill's diplomatic comment when confronted with the ugly baby applies here, all right.

Now, *that* is a pharaoh!

Fortunately there were others, including his father, with more brains and more real accomplishments to give substance to the trade. But of its most ubiquitous and egotistical practioner one can truly say:

That Ramesses! He *was* a pharaoh!

You can bet your uraeus he was.

Some one hundred and eighty years later his distant namesake, Ramesses III, was buried in the Valley of the Kings in the tomb which is second only to Seti's in size and grandeur. He was the last Ramesses, of the twelve of that name, to possess any real stature and achievement—both substantially greater than those of our friend of Abu Simbel—and he was also relatively modest about it. He did vastly expand the ancient temple of Medinet Habu and rededicate it with his throne name, "The House of Millions of Years of King User-ma-Ra Meri-Amon Possessed of Eternity in the House of Amon," and on its walls at extensive and repetitive length he did recount his major victories over the Mediterranean peoples who attempted to invade Egypt, along with all his other successful campaigns to protect the Two Lands. But aside from that, he was content to let the record, which was generally admirable, stand.

Perhaps the wealthiest of all the pharaohs, he gave great gifts to the priesthoods of Amon, Mut, Khonsu and all the other gods of Thebes; to Atum, Ra-Herakhte and the other gods of Heliopolis; to Ptah and Sekhmet and the other gods of Memphis, "as well as all the good benefactions for the people of the land of Egypt and every land, to unite them all together..."

In the accounts of his gifts to each set of deities there is a recurring theme whose poignancy the visitor does not realize until he visits one of the smaller tombs of the Valley of the Queens, in the stark hills a quarter mile west of Medinet Habu. It then becomes clear why virtually the same appeal is made to each of the gods in turn, and, finally, to the people themselves.

"Hear my petition!" he cries to Amon, to Ptah, to all the rest. "Crown my son as king upon the throne of Atum, establish him as Mighty Bull, Lord of the Two Shores, King of Upper and Lower Egypt, Lord of the Two Lands, User-ma-Ra Set-e-pen-Amon (Life, Prosperity, Health), Son of Ra, Lord of Diadems, Ramesses [IV] Hekma-meri-Amon... Give to him a reign of millions of years... Make him divine more than any king... Make his body to flourish and be youthful daily... Grant for him that Egypt may rejoice, ward off all evil, misfortune and destruction. Give to him joy abiding in his heart, jubilation, singing and dancing before his beautiful face... Give great and rich Niles in his time, in order to supply his reign with plentiful food... Make sound his every limb, make to flourish his bones and eyes, flourishing in beholding the love of millions. Give him satisfying life, united with his limbs, and health for his members at every season... Put the love of him in the hearts of the people, may the whole land acclaim over him at the sight of him, may Egypt rejoice over him with jubilation, united under his feet forever..."

And finally, to the people themselves:

"Be attached to his sandals, kiss the earth in his presence, bow down to him, follow him at all times, adore him, praise him, magnify his beauty as you do to Ra every morning. Present to him your tribute [in] his august palace, bring to him the gifts of the lands and countries. Be zealous for his commissions, the commands which are spoken among you. Obey his behests, that you may prosper under him. Labor for him as one man in every work; transport for him monuments, dig for him canals, do for him the work of your hands, that you may enjoy his favor, in possession of his provisions every day . . ."

He must have greatly loved this son, this capable old man who died in disappointment and dismay after the discovery of the "harem conspiracy" that was meant to kill him and put some other, minor, son upon the throne. It did not succeed. User-ma-Ra Set-e-pen-Amon (Life, Prosperity, Health) Ramesses Hekma-meri-Amon assumed the Double Crown as his father had desired; the old man's prayers were answered. It is in the Valley of the Queens, in the most humanly touching of all the tombs of the necropolis, that the visitor finds the reason for the desperate urgency of his supplications.

There was another son; and while there is no indication in the records where he stood in the line of Ramesses' children, it seems a fair presumption that Amon-hir-khop-shef was the firstborn of Pharaoh and his doting father fully expected him to succeed in due time to the kingship of the Two Lands.

It was not to be. The boy died at nine of some cause we are not told in the tomb. The evidence of a poignant grief speaks across almost three millennia as strongly as though it were yesterday.

An extraordinary honor was paid this boy, who still wears the sidelock of youth. In colors and detail still as bright as when they were first put on the walls, Pharaoh himself is shown leading his son to judgment in the afterworld; the only living Pharaoh, save Aye with Tutankhamon, who is shown in one of the tombs participating directly in the rites of death. Amonhirkhopshef was obviously a very special son of Ramesses III, for no other pharaonic son has been found so honored and protected on his way to face the gods. There is an importance about it, and a tenderness, that still have the capacity to move.

The boy carries the feather of truth of the goddess Ma'at. Ramesses strides on protectively ahead as he takes his son to meet the gods.

The boy's mummy was not found in the sarcophagus. In its place someone in the unknowable past had placed a six-month fetus, which is still preserved in one corner of the burial chamber in a small glass case. Whether this was the result of a miscarriage by the grieving mother—whether it was some grave robber's superstitious attempt to make amends for his desecration—no one knows, or likely will ever know.

The tomb, with its tender representation of father and son, says much about Ramesses III: a pharaoh, obscured by his flashier predecessors, who perhaps deserves more credit than he gets from those who dismiss his lengthy lists and prayers at Medinet Habu as just more royal boasting. It would appear that there was considerably more to him than that.

It is now, however, getting on toward late afternoon. Ra is beginning to hasten toward his barque in the west, the shadows of the peak where Mertseger lives are falling across the haunted valleys. In his tomb Tut sleeps alone; all about him lie emptiness and silence. It is time to return to the landing stage, take the wheezing launch, return to the pleasures of Luxor—the predinner libation to the gods for getting one through another hot day; dinner at the hotel or the arcade restaurant— the good bread, the tahini to dip it in, the bottle of Omar Khayyam red wine, the inevitable lamb or beef or fish; the brightly lighted bustle of the busy main street, still swarming with life, if one cares to go walking afterward; the shadowy tree-lined waterfront where enterprising young vendors and felucca drivers still offer their wares as night draws on.

Nakht, User-het, Menna, Rekh-mi-ra and Ra-mo-se await tomorrow in the necropolis. Now it is time to relax and let the peace of Luxor, and of Thebes, restore the body and the soul.

Once more the wheezing launch, once more Hapi's broad, swift-flowing bosom, once more the sellers waiting on the western bank; once more the glare of noon. Again, it is near-deserted as we arrive. A couple of taxis still wait. We drive on out across the fields, past the modern government-built, empty village of el-Qurna where the enterprising descendants of the grave robbers refuse to live, past the stumpy ruins of the colossi of Amonhotep III, to the old village of el-Qurna, snuggled in among the Tombs of the Nobles, in the soft, crumpled hills at the feet of the craggy mountains that climb to the Peak of the West. Legend says the villagers have these mounds and tombs so thoroughly honeycombed with tunnels that beneath every mud-house there is an entryway to the afterworld of the nobles. But it is not the gods' afterworld that is entered. It is the afterworld of the occasional genuine scarab or genuine necklace, the occasional genuine gold or faience statuette of Thoth or Ma'at or Horus that still finds its way secretly to Luxor or downriver to the great bazaar of Khan el-Khalili in Cairo.

Three tombs tell much of the daily life of the Ancients, even though that life is seen here, as is characteristic, through the lens of the nobles. Among the more than three hundred noble tombs that cluster the slopes of el-Qurna, three are typical of the many that lead us into a lively and human world—those of Nakht, scribe of the granaries under Tuthmose IV, User-het, royal scribe to Amonhotep II, and Menna, scribe of the fields under Tuthmose IV.

It is notable here that it is not only in Akhenaten's Amarna that the visitor finds the "naturalistic" art that distinguishes his reign and is made so much of by some commentators. It is true that the naturalistic portrayals he caused to be made of himself, Nefertiti and their six daughters are unusual for a pharaoh; but as far back as the Old Kingdom tombs in Sakkara near Cairo one can find portrayals of daily life so natural, realistic and charming that they could be plucked out and set down in the fields today and be perfectly at home. Paintings and carvings of Pharaoh, the gods, battles, state and religious occasions, all had their rigid rules that continue from generation to generation without break save Akhenaten's—the full frontal view of the body, the face turned in profile. Statues had similar conventions, the arms held rigid at the sides or crossed holding crook and flail, one foot positioned ahead of the other, face straight ahead, the smile usually on the lips. All other Egyptian art was, from the beginning, simple, natural, unafraid to show human beings doing human things. In the tombs of the nobles, and in the many stone and wooden representations of daily life that have come down to us, artists were free to picture things as they were. Akhenaten's "artistic revolution" was revolutionary for a pharaoh; it was not revolutionary in terms of a very sizable portion of Egyptian art.

The tombs of Nakht, Userhet and Menna are small like those of most nobles, but their paintings are among the best preserved, and most detailed, in the entire necropolis. The artists obviously enjoyed what they were doing. Whenever there was chance to include a human detail, they put it in.

Many of the tombs in the Valley of the Nobles carry charming depictions of the day-by-day life of Ancient Egypt. One of the most beautiful shows a funeral procession with pall-bearers, servants carrying relics of the deceased, and women of the household weeping for the honored dead. On a more cheerful note, another painting shows some of the birds and animal life which the Ancients loved to be surrounded by, and hunt.

There are scenes of agriculture: plowing, digging, sowing, reaping, measuring, winnowing the grain and pressing it into baskets. One laborer is so enthusiastic that he is leaping into the air so that his body will have greater impact in tamping down the grain. A plowman has scraggly hair and another fellow off under a tree is surreptitiously taking a nip of wine to fortify himself against the heat of the day.

In Nakht's tomb appear the famous nude "three dancing girls," favorites of so many tourist postcards—a lute player dances to the accompaniment of harpist and flautist. Above, a blind harpist plays to a group of women who are paying no attention to the dancers but seem to be gossiping among themselves. A naked girl is leaning down to hold a pot of perfume to the nostrils of three of the women. Nakht's cat growls beneath his chair to protect some stolen morsel.

Nakht's small daughter, in a delightfully natural pose, is shown hiding behind his leg while he shoots birds and spears fish. Menna's daughter watches him from among the rushes while he stalks game. Servants, which all noblemen had, are catching birds in nets, harvesting grapes, making wine. Two girls quarrel, another carefully removes a thorn from the foot of a friend.

In the tomb of Userhet, royal scribe to Amonhotep II, there is a feast scene, all of whose feminine figures were defaced many centuries ago by a Christian monk who used the tomb as living quarters and obviously did not approve of naked women. But other scenes remain intact. In one, a man is bringing bags of gold dust to be counted. In another a queue of men is waiting for the barber, already at work on not one but two clients. Bakers bake bread. Userhet makes offerings to Amonhotep II, who wears an unusual red tunic with yellow spots. There is a hunting scene in which Userhet, reins around his waist so that his hands are free to hold his bow taut and ready, dashes through the marshes in his chariot hunting jackals, hares, gazelles and other wildlife. Other scenes show viticulture, fishing, fowling. Finally, funerary scenes depict weaping women sorrowing for Userhet, who at that point has evidently departed for the afterworld.

Out of all this pleasant life of planting, harvesting, fishing, fowling, hunting and out of the many tombs and texts that record it have come those statements, some narrative, some poetry, that bring the Ancients to vivid life.

Tart social advice, such as:

"Don't start drinking, because if you speak, something else will come out of your mouth. You won't know what you are saying. You will fall down and break your limbs. Nobody will take you by the hand. Your drinking companions will stand apart and say: Look at that drunkard! If someone comes to look for you, to ask your advice, he will find you lying on the floor, like a little baby."

Advice on a career, such as:

"Be a scribe, who is freed from forced labor, and protected from all work. He is released from hoeing with the hoe, and you need not carry a basket. It separates you from plying the oar, and it is free from vexation. You do not have many masters, or a host of superiors.

"No sooner has a man come forth from his mother's womb than he is defenseless before his superior...

"But the scribe, he directs every work that is in this land."

Advice to the teacher:

"A boy's ears are on his back, and he listens when he is beaten."

Advice to the young man:

"Beware of a woman from abroad, who is not known in her city. She is like the vortex of deep waters, whose whirling no one can fathom. The woman, whose husband is far away, she writes to you every day. If there is no one to see, she arises and spreads her net. O deadly crime, if one responds!"

Love songs in which the singers refer to one another as "my brother" and "my sister," including such excerpts as:

The girl—

"My brother, it is pleasant to go to the water in order to bathe myself in your presence, that I may let you see my beauty in my tunic of finest royal linen when it is wet... I go down with you into the water and come forth again to you with a red fish lying beautiful on my fingers... Come and look at me... If you desire to caress my thigh, my breast will beckon you... Take my breast; what it has overflows for you... Most good it is to go to the meadow to him who is beloved... Fairest one, my desire shall be that I love you as your wife, that your arm be laid upon my arm... How pleasant is my hour! Might an hour only become for me eternity, when I sleep with you..."

The boy (perhaps slightly more practical)—

"I see my sister coming and my heart rejoices. My arms are opened wide to embrace her, and my heart rejoices upon its place when she comes to me... Ah, would I were her negress that is her handmaid, then would I behold the color of all her limbs... Ah, would I were her signet ring... If I embrace her and her arms are opened, it is as though I were one that is from Punt, smelling her unguent... If I kiss her and her lips are open, I am drunk even without beer..."

And, finally, very often, that bittersweet vision of mortality, found in so many different forms in so many texts but basically the same, sung at so many banquets one finds pictured on the walls:

"Bodies pass away and others come in their place, since the time of them that were before.

"The gods that were aforetime rest in their pyramids, and likewise the noble and the glorified are buried in their pyramids.

"They that build houses, their habitations are no more. What has been done with them?... Their walls are destroyed, their habitations are no more, as if they had never been...

"None comes from thence to tell us how they fare, to tell us what they need, to set our hearts at rest until we also go to the place where they are gone.

"Be glad, that you may cause your heart to forget that men will one day glorify you at your funeral. Follow your desire, so long as you live. Put myrrh on your head, clothe yourself in fine linens and anoint yourself with the marvels of life.

"Increase yet more the delights that you have and let not your heart grow faint. Follow your desire and do good to others and yourself. Do what you must upon earth and vex not your heart, until that day of lamentations comes to you: for He with the Quiet Heart, Great Osiris, hears not lamentations, and cries deliver no man from the underworld.

"Spend the day happily and weary not thereof!

"Lo, none can take his goods with him!

"Lo, none that has departed can come again!"

Many tombs, many dead, here in el-Qurna where the elders seek to sell their goods and the children hover in fierce, hawklike little groups around sometimes frightened lady tourists: a harsh landscape and, for Egypt, a harsh people, conditioned, like their ancestors before them immemorial, to the defiance of authority and the insistent intimidation of the visitor. A closed society, el-Qurna, sitting atop who knows what remaining treasures? Its people, if they do know, are not going to let you find out unless the knowledge can be turned to profit for them.

Among the sandy hummocks, bare and harsh at the foot of the brooding hills, is perhaps the most important nonroyal tomb in the Two Lands, that of Rekh-mi-ra, vizier and "governor of the residence" during the closing years of Tuthmose III and the opening years of his son, Amonhotep II. The pleasant folk who live on in such tombs as those of Nakht, Userhet, Menna, the writers of the love poems, the "instructions" and the other papyri that have survived to us, needed governance; and in a country whose population has been estimated at around 5,000,000 for most of its long history, Pharaoh could not do it all. Very early in the dynastic age there began to be a division of powers, the gradual establishment of officials to tend to the day-to-day, Pharaoh remaining the ultimate ruler and final appeal. The many scenes in Rekhmira's tomb provide the most extensive remaining catalogue of the duties and responsibilities that devolved upon the official who was, second only to Pharaoh himself, the most powerful man in the kingdom.

He knew it, too. An opening inscription announces that he was "a noble, second to the king. There was nothing of which he was ignorant, in heaven, in earth, in any quarter of the netherworld." In this he associates himself completely with the king, who "knew that which occurred, there was nothing which he did not know, he was Thoth in everything, there was no affair whch he did not complete."

There follows a lengthy and rather haphazard list of duties which give a vivid picture of all the responsibilities the vizier had. Even a partial recounting indicates that they must have taxed the capabilities of even one as self-confident as Rekhmira:

"The going-out of all that goes out of the king's court shall be reported to him, and the coming in of all that comes into the court shall be reported to him." His messengers alone shall conduct visitors in and out of the king's private chambers. He shall go in to take counsel with the king on the affairs of the Two Lands, and their affairs shall be reported to him each day. . . He shall keep the criminal docket of all pending cases and a record of the disposition of all cases.

District officials may be appointed by the vizier and are responsible to him. Every property list or will is brought to him and is not official until he places his seal upon it. He shall administer tenant lands in all the districts and shall decide boundary disputes. . . Officials of the northern and southern frontiers, and of the holy precincts of Abydos, shall report to him, in person and in writing, all their activities on the first day of each of the three four-month periods into which the calendar is divided.

He organizes Pharaoh's household troops whenever the king goes north or

Rekhmira was vizier, or principal administrative officer, for Tuthmose III. This powerful hand represents the strength, dignity and unassailable certainty with which he and other viziers down the millennia conducted the daily business of government for the god-kings they served.

south. He is in charge of garrisoning the residence in the king's absence. He issues the regulations of the army and navy . . .

Every official in the land "from first to last" is required to consult the vizier in the performance of his duties. He orders the felling of trees according to the decision of the court. He dispatches the official staff to supervise the water supply for the entire country. He tells the mayors and village sheiks when it is time to plow. He appoints overseers of labor in the court. He arranges audiences for mayors and sheiks of villages. He sets the boundaries of every nome (political district) and keeps the records of every nome's divine offerings and contracts.

He appoints judges for special cases. He receives a record of all offerings made to the gods and levies all income taxes. It is he who inspects and records all foreign tribute. He inspects the canals in the residence city every ten days. He receives reports monthly from every district supervisor and overseer so that he will know how to collect tribute from the districts fairly.

There are numerous scenes of Rekhmira supervising every possible daily activity in Egypt, which, unless he were slightly more superhuman than even the officials of Ancient Egypt liked to consider themselves, would have required a seventy-two-hour day and a fourteen-day week.

Nonetheless, out of his listings there emerges the best picture we have of the highly organized government of Egypt in the days of its greatest glory, the Eighteenth Dynasty. There seems little doubt that the vizier did indeed supervise most of these activities. If so, he must have had a civil service to assist him almost as top-heavy as the priesthood of Amon; and the attitude of the average citizen toward it must have been exactly the same as that of the average citizen of Cairo — or America — or wherever — today: government is too big, too costly, too wasteful. Now, at least, the citizen can occasionally if futilely protest. There was no protest then: the vizier's power came directly from Pharaoh, and Pharaoh was absolute.

Much depended, therefore, upon the character of the man chosen. Rekhmira, like some of the other great viziers and favorites who were given power during the good times, seems to have been a diligent and honorable man. There would be viziers later, in the time of twilight, who would attempt to seize the throne, other favorites who would subvert and betray Pharaoh and impose great hardships on the people. But Rekhmira seems to have belonged to the great tradition of those officials, viziers and lesser rank, who served faithfully and well and considered themselves fully entitled to boast about it.

None whose voices speak so self-confidently across the millennia had quite the problem of the man whose tomb is probably the most beautiful in the Valley of the Nobles. Ramose, vizier under Amonhotep III and, for a time, Akhenaten, walked a delicate rope. His tomb is both an illustration of the transition period during which Akhenaten was organizing his great revolution against Amon and the other gods, and a preview of what the visitor finds on the haunted plain at Tell el-Amarna.

Ramose, like Rekhmira and everyone else in his position, described himself

Alabaster pillars lead the visitor into the loveliest of the noble tombs, that of Ramose, vizier for Amonhotep III and then for Amonhotep's revolutionary son Akhenaten.

Delicate, serene and perfect, Ramose's children give no sign that they were living through Ancient Egypt's most difficult period.

with no false modesty. Among a number of other things, he was, he tells us, "a doer of truth, a hater of deceit . . . just judge . . . sole companion, whom the Lord of the Two Lands loved because of his remarkable traits . . . the mouth that makes content in the whole land . . . entering into the secrets of heaven, of earth, of the netherworld . . . master of secret things of the palace . . ."

In other words, quite a fellow. He must have been to have successfully ridden the wave of Akhenaten's rebellion from this tomb, which is empty, to the tomb of Ramose at Amarna, also empty but evidently intended for his final resting place.

His tomb at Thebes, like so many others, is quiet, serene and peaceful when the visitor descends the steps and enters the cooling earth; but also like so many others, and like so many inscriptions in the great temples, it is the key to towering passions, raging ambitions and furious contentions. All is peaceful now; but let the imagination roam just a little and we are instantly back in the midst of desperate intrigues and bitter conflicts that could, and did, cost many lives.

Ramose's tomb is the only place in which Akhenaten is shown both before and after his formal establishment of his "Sole God," the Aten. Without this tomb there would still be great uncertainty as to whether Amonhotep IV and Akhenaten were one and the same. Here, there is no doubt.

There are two representations of Pharaoh. The first shows him in conventional style, behind him the goddess Ma'at, in front Ramose hailing him with upraised arms. Pharaoh here is represented in the Amon faith.

Across the tomb, whose broad expanse, stone pillars and delicate alabaster carvings give a sense of spaciousness unusual in the necropolis, is another relief, startling in its contrast. Here the King and Nefertiti, both shown in the typical belly-sagging Amarna style, make offerings to the sun-disk of the Aten, whose spidery arms and tiny hands reach down to confer his blessings upon them. And although Pharaoh is still here styled "Amonhotep," both the pose and the second address by Ramose show that the Aten faith was then already in full tide.

Akhenaten had apparently not yet changed his name. But he had already constructed a temple to the Aten called "Aten-Is-Found-in-the-House-of-Aten"—the "Gem-Aten" whose ruins are now being excavated and restored south of the main temple at Karnak. And Ramose's words to the king leave no doubt of the situation already prevailing:

"You are the Only One of Aten, in possession of all his designs. You have conquered the mountains; the terror of you is in the midst of their secret chambers, as the terror of you is in the hearts of the people; they hearken to you as the people hearken."

The terror of him was indeed in the hearts of the people, for they did not know what to make of this strange Pharaoh who was turning upside down all the gods and two thousand years of tradition. But hearken they did not — and he apparently did not really care—and therein lies much of the tragedy of Akhenaten . . .

Now Ra speeds swiftly down the sky beyond the Peak of the West. A lovely, gentling purple light lies on the forbidding hills among which so many strong and dominant personalities sought their final rest. Along the green fields at river's edge a soft haze lies as the black-swathed village women come down to collect water for the evening meal. A few cattle graze. Here and there smoke rises from peasant huts. Homecoming feluccas drift toward the Luxor shore. The Nile deepens through gold to bronze to black. Peace lies upon the land. Passions, ambitions, contentions are muted now: even their memory is, for a little while, at rest. The necropolis sleeps.

It is time to turn to Karnak and the Temple of Luxor before we head on north to Tell el-Amarna, Cairo, Alexandria, Giza, Sakkara, the Old Kingdom, the Museum, and journey's end.

It is probably the world's most impressive *Son et Lumière* —but, after all, look at the material they have to work with. The two-thousand-year jumble of Karnak, jagged temples and halls and obelisks and walls and archways, detritus of two millennia and perhaps as many as a hundred pharaohs great and small, known and unknown, whose architects, artisans and workers labored here on a monument whose creation did not cease until the last hammer fell, sometime early in the Christian era. No one knows when the exact moment came, nor do we know with exactitude which of the pharaohs contributed many of the infinite details that embellish the constantly unfolding vistas through which the visitor walks bemused by the message of the Ancients.

It is the message of Amon true enough; but more than that it is the message of *power*. Amon's power. Thebes' power. The Double Crown's power. The power of individual pharaohs who built here, such as Tuthmose III, Hatshepsut, Amonhotep III, Akhenaten, Horemheb, Seti I, Ramesses II and III, Taharka and the rest.

These little people built so very, very big, for reasons a modern psychologist might define in a moment's glib comparison of their size and their buildings' size. Yet browsing through Karnak, as the wise visitor takes time to do, it is obvious that there was much more to it than that. It was not entirely, or even partially, perhaps, that, being little, they wished to build big. It has much more to do with their vision of themselves and their gods in the world as they knew it. No one had greater power and glory: no one deserved more splendid recognition. And very few in all history, it seems safe to say, received as much, or even near it.

To this the *Sound and Light* pays more than adequate tribute. Indeed, the tribute begins before the performance, because there is always a certain excitement in the air around the hotels in early evening. The visitors swarm out, pile in, some few in taxis or buses but by far the greater number in the horse carriages which now come into their glory. Now one meets Mohammed or Abrahim or Mahmoud, usually accompanied by a small enormous-eyed son, very anxious that you should remember his name and carriage number, because that is all you will have to go on when you emerge an hour and a half later from two thousand years of history into the clutter of carriages and shouting drivers who fill the space before the temple.

The carriage proceeds, usually at a placid and steady trot, north along the river, first through the lighted area of the hotels, then along a darker stretch past Chicago House, where the earnest and hardworking young professors of that university center their continuing research; past the delightful little Luxor Museum, perfectly designed and lighted showcase for a small and carefully selected exhibit of some of Egypt's most stunning antiquities; and so presently, with a right turn off the corniche, along perhaps another half mile of shaded street that indicates the river's shift away from the temple complex over the millennia.

So one arrives at the ancient landing stage and there before one are the First Pylon and the avenue of ram-headed sphinxes, representing Amon in his form of the ram. Each ram bears on its forehead the disk of the sun, and each holds between its paws a statue of—one could never guess—Ramesses II, who ordered this avenue constructed so that the very first thing one encounters when coming from the river side of Karnak is a memento of him.

The lion bodies of the sphinxes represent Amon's strength; the expression of the ram faces can be interpreted variously. Some observers profess to find them benign in expression. To others they appear to be cold—very cold. Cold and arrogant and all-dominating and completely heartless, which, after all, is what Amon was. They are not friendly, these rams: they are cruel and superior and they want you to know it. There is no slightest appeal, one feels, from that smug and arrogant expression; and while perhaps all rams look that way, in their dullard stupidity and stubbornness, still here, where they are intended to represent the King of Gods in the temple which was known as "The Throne of the World," something more deliberately and knowingly intimidating seems to enter in.

But that, of course, may be oversentimentalizing: perhaps they are just there to symbolize a gentle "Baa, baa!" of greeting to the visitor. This is not like Amon, but maybe so. In any event, their double row, stretching down a slight incline into the great Amon temple, is impressive at any time. It becomes doubly so when, at the appointed hour, all lights are suddenly doused and then brought slowly and most effectively up again upon their waiting ranks as the pleasant feminine voice says, "Welcome, O travelers to Upper Egypt! You are in the House of the Father."

In his house we are, but interestingly enough, historically at the backdoor; for this temple, unlike some in Egypt, was built originally from the east to the west, not the other way around. And in truth, of all the major ones, only Abu Simbel seems to have been consciously orientated to face the sun, so that its first rays fall upon Pharaoh and the gods within. More were built like Edfu, whose inscription reads: "I gripped the wooden stake and the handle of the scepter. I held the string with the goddess Seh-sat; my eyes followed the course of the stars and rested on Mes-het the Great Bear; the god who controls time stood near my *mrkt* [hourglass]. I established the limitations of the four corners of the temple."

In similar fashion, in the Karnak complex, the temple of Mut, Amon's wife, faces north and that of his son Khons or Khonsu faces south. The sun was worshipped but he was apparently felt to be in every direction.

Thus the Amon temple began originally far back in the center of the area toward which the visitors walk as the presentation proceeds—in the sanctuary, tiny in all the towering masonry around it, which is illuminated in red as the talk begins. Seen in daylight later when one comes to wander and ruminate, it appears at first a very small, not every impressive, space. But from it sprang all this vast complex and two thousand years of domination over Egypt. It carries a weight of history infinitely larger than its size.

Approaching it as one does, the "First Pylon" actually is one of the last, built by the Nubians when they came up from below the Fourth Cataract in the dying years to rule the land that for so long had ruled them. The children of wretched

"The two-thousand-year jumble of Karnak, jagged temples and halls and obelisks and walls and archways, detritus of two millennia and perhaps as many as a hundred pharaohs great and small, known and unknown, whose architects, artisans, and workers labored here on a monument whose creation did not cease until the last hammer fell, sometime early in the Christian era ... Power—power—POWER. Here Amon had it ... So much— so much."

Part of the great cache of more than seven hundred statues discovered in a single burial-place within the walls of Karnak, unknown pharaohs and the ubiquitous ram figure of the god Amon stand watch along the walls.

Kush, Egyptianized many centuries before, knew their duty to the god when they came to power. Their pylon was never finished, but its massive walls are quite impressive enough as a gateway to the vast constructions that lie beyond.

The first of these, called now "the Great Court," was also built very late, in the Twenty-second Dynasty. Within its walls on the right is a modest little temple built by Ramesses III at the end of the continuation of the row of sphinxes that was interrupted by the First Pylon. On the left, immediately after the pylon, diagonally across from Ramesses is the small three-chambered shrine to Amon, Mut and Khonsu built by Seti II. Extending on from it are the remaining sphinxes of the left-hand row. Miscellaneous pedestals and colonnades bear the names of Psamtik II of the Twenty-sixth Dynasty, who, pre-empting a predecessor as many a pharaoh did, had his cartouche inscribed over that of the Nubian Taharka. Ptolemy IV is also recorded there. The ruins of brick ramps still remain against the inner wall of the First Pylon, indicating that stones and columns were raised in this fashion — as, insofar as most probable evidence indicates, were the pyramids.

Passing through the Great Court the visitor comes next to the Hypostyle Hall, that most overwhelming of enclosed spaces, its 134 columns arranged in 16 rows, their tops purportedly able to hold 100 men—though which 100, or when, one is never told. It's a handy figure, however, and it is certain that innumerable tourists can verify that it does take a dozen or so, arms outstretched and fingertips touching, to embrace the base of each pillar. Originally roofed, the hall was found in sad tumbledown decay by Napoleon's expedition in 1798, and its restoration, completed in 1956 by a group of French Egyptologists working under contract for the Department of Antiquities, has left it sans roof but otherwise much as it stood originally. It was begun by Ramesses I, greatly expanded by Seti I. The relatively small southern portion necessary to complete it was built by Ramesses II, who of course took credit for the whole thing. In addition to the one-hundred-men-on-a-pillar cliche, the visitor is also told that the dimly lit jungle of stone in which he is standing could comfortably accommodate the entire cathedral of Notre Dame, which is true.

Beyond the Great Court, one passes the Third Pylon, built by Amonhotep III at about the same time he was building the Temple of Luxor, and the Fourth, built by Tuthmose I; beyond it the famous colonnade, originally a hall, where Tuthmose III was chosen by Amon, which Hatshepsut later tore to pieces so that she might erect her obelisks, and where Tuthmose III in due time returned to erect his spite-wall so that nobody could see them. This leads through two more small pylons, a colonnade, and so to the site of the original sanctuary, lost in antiquity but given its present form in the small, two-chambered structure built by Philip Arrhidaeus, brother of Alexander the Great.

In the second of these small rooms stood on his pedestal above the abject worshipper the original gold Amon. Each morning, as with all his gold-plated duplicates at Luxor and all the other smaller temples throughout the Two Lands, he was taken down by reverent priests, carefully washed, anointed with oils and perfumes,

The avenue of ram-headed sphinxes, representing the god, welcomes the visitor to the great temple and to the holy of holies, the tiny sanctuary far at the end in which Amon-Ra's golden statue stood.

Once-proud houses for the gods gape in a ruined jumble beneath Egypt's almost always sunny sky.

Only the constant efforts of archeologists and the Egyptian Government keep back the ever-encroaching sands, the never-resting weeds that threaten again to cover Karnak.

clothed and had his face made up—a ceremony duplicated by Pharaoh in his palace to show his respect for, and identity with, the god. Amon was then placed back on his pedestal and further chantings and rituals were conducted by the priesthood. At their conclusion he was taken down, disrobed, washed carefully again and placed once more upon his pedestal. The day in the Two Lands was now properly begun.

Beyond and on both sides proliferate further temples, shrines, colonnades, avenues, but this is the essential heart of Karnak insofar as Amon was concerned. There is no firm explanation for the division into pylon—great court—hypostyle hall—colonnade—sanctuary which characterized Karnak and so many Egyptian temples. Some theorize that it was due to the social divisions of the kingdom, so that the peasants were admitted to the Great Court and then, as the structures narrowed down, so too did the social classes which were permitted to enter each successive one, until finally only Pharaoh and the High Priest of Amon and his immediate attendants could enter the sanctuary.

This explanation is reasonably satisfactory and probably did have a good deal to do with it. Even more fundamental, one suspects, was the creation of a deliberate series of blows to the mind, so that at each step one became more overwhelmed with the power of Amon, more closed in, more oppressed by the steadily deepening atmosphere of shadow and gloom—until finally when one came, if one was Pharaoh the supreme One, to the sanctuary, the psychological impact of Amon's golden statue, lit only by a single ray of sunlight falling artfully on his somber face from a slit high in the roof, must have been awesome indeed.

It must have taken all the certainty of the knowledge of one's own godhood to face him then; and it is only when one enters these precincts, passes through and then looks back from across the Sacred Lake at all the great jumble of buildings and power that were AMON that one realizes the fantastic and almost unbelievable courage of the one malformed, misshapen but indomitable pharaoh who dared to challenge him.

Today, like Hatshepsut before him, he is in process of having the last word; not that he ever really did not have it, no matter how vigorously his successors tried to destroy his memory. But he is having it within the complex of Karnak itself, which has its ironies. His temple to the Aten at Karnak is being restored.

In due course, as funds become available, the Gem-Aten will rise once more within the precincts of Karnak. It is possible that this may reveal with certainty much about the Amarna period that is only guesswork now. Certain it is that it will give "the Heretic" his last, ironic triumph, when Aten's temple stands finally restored, side by side with Amon's.

Amon's name first appears in Thebes in the First Intermediate Period, c. 2181—2050 B.C., and according to an inscription his first temple, long since completely lost, was built there at about that time. It was not until the Twelfth Dynasty, however, that serious building on the Karnak site began, and this was done by Amenemhet I, founder of the dynasty. His son Sesostris I left the earliest known

It is said that a hundred men could
stand atop one of the columns in
the Great Hypostyle Hall at
Karnak. Certainly generations of
tourists know that it takes at least
a dozen of them with linked arms
to reach around the circumference.

Across the Sacred Lake, present-day excavators still work patiently among the jumble of the past, almost daily uncovering new aspects of the enormous complex which is Karnak.

remains which have been found, a sanctuary in the center of what presently became the great central temple. Sesostris also built the perfect little pavilion that stands outside the northern wall of Karnak. With typical courtesy of one pharaoh to another, Amonhotep III ripped it up and used its blocks to build the Third Pylon. Sesostris, too, has a last word, however, for in 1937—38 his pavilion was restored to its original form and place and now may be visited with special permission. It is very simple, chaste, modestly adorned.

Equally exquisite is the small temple of Ptah which lies almost directly east of it a few hundred yards. There Ptah's wife, the lion-headed goddess Sekhmet, sits in black granite in a tiny room, a single ray of sunlight falling on her impassively forbidding and beautiful face—perhaps the most impressive of all her many representations and certainly one of the most stunning statues in all of Egypt.

Amonhotep III was one of the greatest builders at both Karnak and Luxor. His architect, builder and closest adviser, who is always referred to by the virtual title "Amonhotep, Son of Hapu," was the only private citizen in Egyptian history who was given the privilege of building his own mortuary temple in royal precincts, in Medinet Habu, and one of the handful deified in later dynasties. With his aid Amonhotep III built an extensive temple to the goddess Mut, wife of Amon, south of the main temple and decorated it with some six hundred statues of Sekhmet, who was also, in that casual conglomerative way of Egyptian mythology, a representation of Mut (which made her wife of Amon as well as wife of Ptah, if one wants to be logical about it. But she wasn't Amon's wife, so why try to be logical?).

There has been much speculation as to why Pharaoh lavished such particular adoration upon Mut. One simple if sentimental explanation might be that his mother, that strong lady, honored the goddess in the name "Mutemwaya" which she took when she came from Mittani to marry Tuthmose IV.

Amonhotep III also loved scarabs, and his scarabs were bigger than anybody's—sometimes four feet in diameter. One, honoring the combined god Atum-Kheperu, stands at one corner of the Sacred Lake, on whose far side the Sound and Light audiences gather in modern stone bleachers to watch the lights rise and fall on the glorious jumble of Karnak as the story concludes. All the dogs of Luxor howl in the night in response to the stately voices, trumpets and drums that accompany the concluding portions of the tale of the temple.

Power—*power*—POWER. Here Amon had it, for two thousand years and more. Here he made and broke pharaohs, controlled the Double Crown from virtually a double kingship, levied with Pharaoh's compliance what must have been a crushing burden on many of Egypt's millions down the centuries. Yet while they must have complained bitterly many times, they must also have done so furtively, for they never rebelled. And when Akhenaten attempted to lead them away from Amon, they were puzzled, frightened, dismayed—and came right back to him the minute Akhenaten vanished from the scene. Such was the hold of the King of the Gods. Here in this vast stone beehive, emptied now of its priests but refilled daily and nightly with visitors from all over the world, resided the greatest continuous power in the Two Lands. Pharaohs came and went, both with Amon's assistance; but Amon went on until the twilight finally fell and, in the closing dynasties, even he could not hold Egypt together. But it was an amazing span of religious power, and Karnak its embodiment is still an amazing place. So much—*so much*. It overwhelms and intimidates still, as it was always meant to do.

Luxor Temple, standing now between hotels at Nile-side near the center of Luxor, impressive by day, beautifully lighted at night, is a smaller, much milder sort of temple. It too was dedicated to Amon, and his annual visit there from Karnak, two miles downriver, was of course the occasion for the grand and glorious bash of Opet. But there is something about the temple of Luxor which seems to reflect its original builder. Amonhotep III—"The Magnificent"—was basically a relaxed, amiable and easygoing man. Luxor Temple in its relatively intimate size becomes him; although Ramesses II—who else?—made a lot of massive additions and made sure a lot of statues of himself were scattered about where no one could miss them.

Like Karnak, Luxor was built on the site of a small Twelfth Dynasty temple. Tuthmose III had placed three small granite shrines there, but little else remained when his great-grandson and Amonhotep, Son of Hapu, went to work.

They rebuilt the original sanctuary, renovated and expanded the chambers that parallel it on each side and placed before it a forecourt of slender columns topped with a papyrus-bud design. A second court was designed and started but Amonhotep III died before its completion. He inaugurated the first festivals of Opet. Then came Akhenaten and the temple underwent the first of many changes.

At his direction all the statues were removed, all references to the pantheon, particularly to Amon, were chiseled out—to the point where even the first portion of his father's name was defaced in the royal cartouches. Opet was cancelled, the priesthood disbanded. Akhenaten went off to Amarna and did not return. For twelve years the Luxor Temple stood empty and deserted on the shore.

When Tutankhamon, under the careful supervision of Aye and Horemheb, returned to Thebes on his brother's death, the rededication of the temple to Amon was begun. Walls were built on each side of the unfinished court, extensive reliefs were placed on the new walls proclaiming Amon's revived glory. Seti I continued the worship of the god, honored Opet, by then a firmly re-established annual tradition, but made no further additions to the building. Along came his son, and things began to hum.

Ramesses II built a much larger colonnaded court in front of the old one, which gives the temple a stepped-up appearance from the river, starting relatively low with Amonhotep III's original papyrus-bud colonnade, rising a level with his first columned court or hypostyle hall, then rising still further with the emphatic if not particularly delicate addition by Ramesses. Ramesses, pausing only long enough to have Tuthmose's cartouches chiseled out of the three small original shrines and replaced with his own, then built a huge entrance pylon, with two obelisks and six

A resident of present-day Luxor hurries past the ruins of the Temple of Luxor, smaller, more modest, in a sense more manageable in the mind than the fantastic hodgepodge of Karnak. Amonhotep III began the major building on the site of a much earlier and smaller temple, but Ramesses II completed it later and characteristically took credit for the whole thing. Inside, as at Karnak, gigantic pillars stretch to the sky in praise of Amon, and of his wife Mut and his son Khonsu, who lived here.

colossal statues of — yes — himself. An inscription proclaims him to be the builder of this entire temple to the glory of Amon.

Along the colonnade which he did build, further colossal statues of himself were put in place, plus two more statues on each side of the doorway, one accompanied by a small statue of Queen Nefertari. The outer face of the pylon is covered with boastful records of his battles with the Hittites, and inside the court the walls contain pictures of his many other wives and a great many of his 150 or so little princes and princesses.

Along the walls enclosing the colonnade built by Amonhotep III are the pictures of Opet put there during Tut's reign. And in a small chamber alongside the sanctuary is Amonhotep's account, inspired by Hatshepsut's at Deir el-Bahri, of his divine birth through the mating of Amon and Queen Mutemwaya.

This was necessary because Amonhotep had a problem somewhat similar to Hatshepsut's. Mutemwaya was not of royal blood — at least not of Egyptian royalty — and therefore his own claim as legitimate heir was in question. One day when he was visiting Deir el-Bahri as an idle tourist more than anything else, he must have hit upon the idea of appropriating Hatshepsut's own concept: he would simply declare himself the divinely conceived child of Amon and that would settle the matter. In jig-time his stonemasons were up there on the walls carving the story of how Amon came to visit Queen Mutemwaya, with Amonhotep the happy result. No sooner carved than done. All was smooth sailing thereafter, and no one ever questioned the legitimacy of Amonhotep III.

Finally, as one moves back through the successive stages of the temple and comes at last to the sanctuary, one comes upon one of the few traces of the Macedonian left in Egypt. Alexander, himself an object of fascination for so many in his own age and later, was fascinated by Egypt and in his brief stay there prior to his death made sure that he too would be associated properly with Amon. He entirely rebuilt the sanctuary, removing the four original columns and replacing them with a shrine. On both inner and outer walls he ordered the carving of reliefs showing himself, complete with cartouche and pharaonic titles, worshipping Amon and the other deities. Even Alexander wanted to be a pharaoh.

But it is the amiable Old-King-Cole-jolly-old-soul personality of Amonhotep III which, despite the bumptiousness of Ramesses II, continues to live most vividly in the Luxor Temple. He was a pleasant fellow, this pharaoh who came to the throne at the very peak of ancient Egypt's glory, when all the Empire was snug and calm, when the holder of the Double Crown had no real worries, when everything conspired to let him coast on the glory of his ancestors — just on the edge of the abyss that was about to be opened by his son.

That he knew the abyss might be coming, there seems little doubt; that in cautious degree he and Queen Tiye encouraged it, there is also little doubt. In the fifth of his famous commemorative scarabs, which records the building of a pleasure lake for her to boat upon, probably in the vicinity of the palace of Malkata on the

The lotus is everywhere, and Karnak furnishes thousands of examples such as this.

204

West Bank, he records the opening day of the lake "when His Majesty sailed thereon in the royal barge: *Aten Gleams.*" The deliberate choice of name, together with other earlier evidence in his reign, indicates that he and Tiye were beginning to lean cautiously in the direction of the Aten as a counterweight to the overweening priesthood of Amon. Their only trouble was that they misread their strange son. What was intended to be modest counterweight became major explosion in his fanatic hands.

Before this cast a saddening pall upon his dying years, however, Amonhotep enjoyed himself with a certain uniquely carefree innocence. Aside from a rebellion in wretched Kush, which he had to put down in the sixth year of his reign, all was peaceful for him. His inscriptions for that battle made up for the remaining peaceful years, however: they made him sound as tough as the best of them, though there is no supporting evidence for his claims that he was a "fierce-eyed lion, he seized wretched Kush, its chiefs were overthrown in their valleys, cast down in their blood, one upon another."

He also claimed that he took a total of 740 "living heads" of Nubians and "312 hands thereof" from the slain, for a total of 1,052 soundly trounced. Another inscription claimed that he had fought in Syria and conquered half a dozen minor principalities in the northeast, but, again, no corroborative evidence has been found.

It is in his commemorative scarabs that his appealing enjoyment of his comfortable life is most evident. A sort of childlike delight and innocence in being pharaoh shines through: the last pharaoh ever to have that carefree an attitude toward his office.

The first scarab commemorates his marriage to Tiye, argued by some to be Nubian but indisputably daughter of two commoners, Yuya and Thuya, whose mummies lie now in the Cairo Museum and certainly are not Nubian.

In the second year of his reign, already married to Tiye, he went on a wild cattle hunt and had such a good time that he issued another scarab to tell all about it.

"Marvel which happened to His Majesty," it begins with a beguiling innocent enthusiasm. "One came to say to His Majesty: 'There are wild cattle upon the highlands as far as the region of *St* [now unknown]. His Majesty sailed downstream in the royal barge *Hmmt* at the time of evening, beginning the goodly way, and arriving in safety in the region of *St* at the time of morning.

"His Majesty appeared upon a horse, his whole army being behind him. The commanders and citizens of all the army in its entirety and the children with them were commanded to keep watch over the wild cattle. Behold, His Majesty commanded to cause that these wild cattle be surrounded by a wall with an enclosure. His Majesty commanded to count all these wild cattle. Account thereof: 170 wild cattle. Statement of the number captured by His Majesty: 56 wild cattle. His Majesty tarried four days" and again "appeared upon a horse. Account of these wild cattle which he captured in the hunt: 26 [plus] wild cattle. 75 [plus] cattle."

In the tenth year of his reign, Amonhotep thought everybody should know how successful he had been in hunting lions. This time the scarab was brief and to the point. After giving his name and titularies, and Tiye's, it says simply:

"Statement of lions which His Majesty brought down with his own arrows from year 1 to year 10: fierce lions, 102."

In Year 10, Amonhotep for reasons of state took another wife, Gil-u-khi-pa of Mittani. Out came another commemorative scarab. In the next year he issued his final scarab, commemorating the building of Tiye's pleasure lake and the significant barge, *Aten Gleams*.

And shortly thereafter he made Akhenaten co-regent and his happy and innocently self-indulgent life ended amid increasing strain and worry about his son, compounded by various physical disabilities that carried him off at a relatively early age somewhere in his late forties.

For the greater part of his reign, however, he enjoyed being pharaoh as none perhaps had before, certainly as none would after. Next only to Ramesses, he was the greatest royal builder. With Tiye he had the happiest marriage. Upon the empire lay the rosy glow of their joint reign. When it slipped into shadow, it slipped very fast. By the time he had completed his building at Luxor Temple the Two Lands were already spinning down into that strange, but strangely moving, darkness from which they would never really recover.

The train to Minya, the city where one stays when visiting Tell el-Amarna, runs all the way from Aswan to Cairo. The visitor coming downriver who wishes to stop off at the site of Akhenaten's city—and increasing numbers seem to, particularly French and Germans—leaves Luxor around ten in the morning, reaches Minya in late afternoon; a long and instructive journey through what is agriculturally the richest part of Egypt. It is also conducive to conversation.

"I hate Cairo," the charming army officer, native of Luxor, said vehemently. "I stay away from there as much as I can. It's too crowded, too dusty, too dirty, too—everything. They don't know how to work there; in fact, they don't know how to work in Egypt anywhere, except on the farms. In the cities they want to stop and take their long lunch hours, they want to come to the office late and leave early; everybody is out to do it the easy way. You can't build a country that way. We've got to be serious about it. It's hard to make people take it seriously."

He stared out for a moment at the passing fields of cotton and sugarcane, while the air-conditioned train, reasonably clean, reasonably comfortable, rocked and rattled over a roadbed not made for too much speed. Occasional groups of workers turned to smile and wave, then turned again to their eternal task. Off to the left, glimpsed now and then among palms and lush green fields, stately felucca sails seemed to float above the ground, sign that Hapi, though obscured by the trees, was keeping us company.

"There is so much to be done. Our population is growing, growing. The government tries, but out here they won't listen. Breeding is a form of social insurance, you know. The younger take care of the older, big families mean security in old age. It is the same all over the world, except in rich countries like yours. And we are not rich. We are very poor...

"It goes deeper than that, though. Here they work because they have to work to stay alive. The heat slows them down, naturally, but they work hard. There isn't the same urgency in the cities. There certainly isn't the same urgency in the government. I suppose civil servants are the same everywhere, but some countries have a bigger margin for laziness and error than we do. The leaders try, but everybody wants his three-hour lunch and his tons of paperwork. Everybody is afraid to take responsibility. So many things that should be done don't get done.

"I suppose on many occasions in the period you're studying"—he smiled—"it was the same. It can't have been all that easy for Pharaoh all the time, either. Human nature doesn't change...except"—he turned serious again—"that they lived in a lot easier world than we do, most of the time. We haven't got three thousand years in which to live down our mistakes. Maybe not even three...

"And then in Cairo it's complicated by the fact that all the young people want to go there, and there are too many people already, and there just aren't enough jobs for everybody, and so you have near-ghettos where there is real urban poverty. People help each other and families stick together just like they do on the land, but prices keep going up and it gets harder and harder. Many don't have jobs. They just hang on . . . somehow.

"I don't know what the solution is. If there is one. But if we keep growing — and we will — . . ." His voice trailed away, he fell silent, eyes somber. A waiter came down the aisle offering Coke, hot tea, beer. "Egypt has got to move," the officer said, ordering tea and with typical Egyptian hospitality insisting on buying one for the visitor, too. "We have got to pull ourselves up by our bootstraps and *move*. But we are defeated by the sheer size of our problems. They wear us down. We are tired out, and our task has really just begun."

(On a higher and more official level that same week in Cairo, Prime Minister Khalil remarked that Egypt was "in a race with time to compensate for past sacrifices by a tired people.")

With this one can sympathize deeply: so many charming, gifted, likable people, struggling — or, in the officer's view, not struggling, depending upon the place in society — against overpopulation, poverty, unemployment, prices not yet rising at a rate comparable with industrialized nations but fast enough to do their damage; plus all the uncertainties of the entire Middle Eastern situation, upon whose solution great hopes are pinned but whose achievement is not so easily at hand. ("Sadat, Carter, Begin, all good men," the shrewd Nubian boy piloting the felucca through the Elephantine Islands at Aswan had declared confidently right after Camp David. "Now we have peace. Peace good. Everybody want peace. Now peace here. Good, good!" As with the Ancients, so now: the word is taken for the deed. But it is not the deed.)

But the green pleasant fields went by, and here, as always with fertile soil — and none is more fertile than Egypt's when the waters of the Nile are placed upon it — it was hard not to think things prosperous when they so richly looked it. Off to the left, out of sight somewhere across the river, we passed the sprawling ruins of Hathor's temple of Dendera, somehow as heavy and cow-like as she, its principal attractions the view over the fields from its remaining roof and the only known Egyptian portrait of Cleopatra, stylized and lifeless, on a wall.

We swung to the left back toward the river, crossed it, began chugging along the west bank, passed, also hidden in the trees, sacred Abydos standing beautiful in the sun. Mud huts, small villages, the daily life—verdant fields, the smiles and waves. The waiter reappeared, bringing lunch, the usual precautions about water were observed: hot tea, as so often in these lands, came to the rescue. Everyone settled back to sleep or read or engage in placid, easygoing conversation. Girga, Balasfura, Sohag, Abu Tig—here and there signs of industry, smokestacks, kilns, an occasional factory. Everywhere the train stopped children jammed dirty fingers, runny noses, great big happy smiles against the windows to wave, exclaim, welcome, laugh at, and with, the foreigners. On parallel tracks the regular commuter trains, old, rusty, open-windowed, crowded to the last inch of space and usually with a few

Along the Nile from Luxor down
to Minya, nearest modern city
to Akhenaten's capital of Tell
el-Amarna, two Egyptian gentlemen
discuss life at their leisure by the
riverbank … and sometimes as far
as the eye can see, fields of cotton,
considered the world's finest, and
sugarcane, both crops going back
to pharaonic times, attest the
richness of the desert when anointed
by Hapi's waters.

The Nile and Egypt's fertile land produce what is generally considered the best cotton in the world, here ready for harvest by hardworking fellahin.

Becoming a major present-day crop along with cotton, sugarcane, like everything else in Egypt, has been known in the land for millennia.

men riding on top of each car, rattled by from time to time. The long thread of life went winding, winding, down the river to Assiut, a big city; then Manfalut, Dairut, Mallawi, Abu Qurqas.

Off to the right across the Nile the cliffs rose a little; empty holes that once were ancient tombs here and there pocked the barren rock. The cliffs swung away in a long, slow curve, came in again. Anticipation rose—there, protected by the river, hidden by trees, was the plain of Akhet-Aten. The train rocked on another thirty miles, the buildings of a substantial city began to appear: Minya, and we were off to our lodging for the two days of our visit to the Heretic's realm.

A horse carriage, to take us the short distance from the railway station. A tiny lobby, behind its desk young fellows who barely spoke English. The tall, perpetually worried, desperately earnest, desperately well-meaning manager. His small, wizened older brother. A tiny lift whose dubious attractions were quickly discarded in favor of the surer process of walking up four flights. The dark eyes of the room boys staring out of the gloom on each landing. The beaming little boy lugging suitcases as big as he. The lumpy beds, the rusty pipes, the barely adequate, frequently broken toilet facilities. The tiny balcony, the view out over the rooftops and abundant trees to the Nile a half mile away. The rushing noise and bustle of Minya's busy life passing the corner night and day. The Hotel Lotus, known to all who ever came to pay their respects to Akhenaten and Nefertiti. Not the Hilton, and not quite the Nefertari, either. Somewhere in between: in its combination of facilities and personnel, rather unique. Certainly not to be forgotten.

216

Connections finally made with a somewhat erratic travel representative, the car and driver duly arrived. Minya is a relatively large city, 100,000 or more, and it took a little while to thread through the crowded streets to the road that runs some thirty miles south to the stone steps and landing dock, quite pharaonic, from which one crosses to the east bank, the little village of Tell el-Amarna and the vast plain of Akhet-Aten. Here, too, there was conversation.

"Egypt have many problems," the driver said, "*many* problems, but at least we better off than when we had that madman we used to have. Nasser, whoosh! He build the dam, he ruin the Nile, all the time war, war, war. Who want war? *We* don't want! Nobody want! We have good man now. Sadat knows we want peace, he try to give it to us. Good man. Good man!"

He had been, it developed, a chemistry student in London until his father died, his family fell on hard times, the money ran out and he had to return to Minya. He was still young, could complete his course here if he really wanted to: the French in particular seem to have made a special project of Minya and maintain good schools there. But—"I got married, and now my wife, the family—better for everybody I drive car, I think. And, no jobs! No jobs! It is hard to find work in Egypt. Egypt need people like me, but no jobs when finish school. Very hard. But"—a sudden cheerful smile, the endless good nature of a hard-pressed, resilient people breaking through—"we all healthy, anyway. Lucky in that, inshallah!"

Which means, "Allah willing," and is heard a thousand times a day.

We drove, horn tooting, brakes squealing, through several sizable towns and villages, humanity and the animal kingdom parting briefly for our passage and then closing again impassively with scarce a ripple left behind. It was a hot morning, dust as always rose from the poorly paved streets; one tried to breathe carefully and endured it. Perhaps twenty-five miles south of Minya we turned left onto a dirt road and began to bear toward the Nile. Across the sugarcane and cotton the fabled cliffs grew closer. Presently we came to a long, straight portion of the road, saw dead ahead the palms and mud huts of a village on the other side; came to the landing area, turned in and parked among the cows and trees. Children, dirty and ragged but generally healthy-looking, scrambled for baksheesh. Their appeals, ranging from noisy cries from the larger to gentle, persistent, almost inaudible mewlings from the smallest, kept us company right down to water's edge.

We stood for a few minutes looking across the river, which flows fast here around a relatively narrow bend, narrower than at Luxor, not so narrow as at Aswan. Water buffalo lay submerged from the heat just off both shores. Upriver a few large feluccas, heavy-laden with produce, tacked against a breath of breeze. Cattle, chickens, donkeys, goats, dogs wandered through the village on the other side. A creaking old motor launch, every bolt complaining, thick oily smoke billowing from an engine that seemed just barely able to make it, crossed and picked us up. We arrived five minutes later on the little rocky promontory where a most unusual pharaoh used to land, 3,300 years ago.

We walked through the village in the company of more begging children, several women selling handsome woven baskets, several village elders commenting loudly to the driver on our little expedition. Jokes, probably at our expense, were exchanged, but not unkindly. After several hundred yards we came to a ramshackle rest house where we were urged to sit for a moment and have a Coke against the heat of the open plain we were about to venture into. We did. Before us lay all that presently remains visible of the fantastic city that was built in perhaps a year or two, complete with palaces, noble homes, workers, houses, shops and bazaars, the living arrangements of several hundred thousand people. It lived, like its ruler, for twelve years after he arrived here; then, like him, it died and was hurried into ruin by the sackings of Horemheb and the implacable vengeance of Amon.

Now there is only desert, unbroken save for a single exception: a new village, constructed perhaps a quarter mile out into the plain. It was built a couple of years ago; it is almost uninhabited now, already itself become a ruin. The government tried to get the residents of Tell el-Amarna to move out there, but they have refused to go.

"They want to stay by the river," the driver explained; but there is likely more to it than that. They also do not want to live in the precincts of the doomed city of Akhet-Aten. Three thousand, three hundred years later it remains a haunted place. Too many ghosts walk here, and the curse of Amon troubles it still in the minds of the superstitious.

And the not-so-superstitious. It takes only a split second for the mind to slip back. There is a sound of horses dashing, a gold-painted carriage rattling over brick cobblestones. Holding the reins is a horse-faced, long-necked, big-bosomed, big-hipped near-caricature of a man wearing a gold crown and uraeus, at his side a beautiful woman (her name, indeed, meaning "A Beautiful Woman is Come") wearing a blue crown, three little girls clinging tightly to her skirts. They rush by with a great dash and clatter, leaving behind startled and wondering looks upon the faces of the crowds whose busy commerce along the streets they have interrupted with their furious, almost insanely intent passage.

Neb-Kheperu-Ra Akhenaten, Lord of the Two Lands, King of the North and South, Mighty Bull, Son of the Sun, his Queen Nefertiti and three of their six daughters have passed. It is one of the wonders of the world to their puzzled people. It is one of the wonders of the world still. What did it all mean?

Scholars and laymen differ, as did his contemporaries. To James Breasted he was "the world's first idealist and the world's first *individual*." To others he was the founder of monotheism whose ideas later were somehow transmitted to the Judaic-Christian world. To others he was a fanatic in pursuit of a goal his people did not understand and were psychologically and intellectually unable to follow. To the desperate clients of the empire, the beleaguered city-states of the Middle East who saw themselves slipping away into the maw of aggressive neighbors as Akhenaten ignored their appeals for help, he was an accident of fate whose obsession with his

Sole God cost them their existence. To Horemheb and his successors, to the priesthoods of Amon and the other gods, and finally to the great majority of his people, he was "the Heretic," "the Criminal of Akhet-Aten," whose works must perish utterly for his sacrilegious attacks upon the pantheon. To no one has he ever been a fully rounded, clearly understood individual, which is why, perhaps, he fascinates us still. No one then, and no one now, has ever really known Akhenaten.

One thing, however, he unchallengeably was, and Breasted sums it up: "a brave soul, undauntedly facing the momentum of immemorial tradition, and thereby stepping out from the long line of conventional and colorless pharaohs, that he might disseminate ideas far beyond and above the capacity of his age to understand."

A brave soul, and undaunted. These, he certainly was.

It is at Karnak that one first realizes this; it is at Amarna that its full import becomes stamped indelibly on the mind. It is a long way from Thebes and Amon, here; and by the sheer power of his personality, fortified it is true by the power of the Double Crown but still attributable above all *to him*, he completely (if temporarily) changed Egypt, and sent forth into the world revolutionary ideas that are living still.

The Aten, and a certain degree of Aten worship, already existed when Akhenaten was born. What he contributed was the idea that there was a *Sole God*, that the Aten embodied it, and that all else must give way before that fact.

The boy who was thus to shake the Two Lands to their depths was born in Malkata, according to generally accepted theory, a normal child. At some point in his early youth he suffered the disease which left him in the misshapen form familiar to all who are interested in the period and to all who have seen the three colossal statues in the Amarna Room of the Cairo Museum. That it also had a profound effect upon his attitude toward the gods seems also a logical conclusion. The ones he prayed to so desperately, particularly the King of the Gods himself, did not answer: they let him suffer. Therefore a human hatred grew, and a desire for vengeance when the time should come for him to assume the Double Crown. Amon was too overweening anyway, and the other gods and their priesthoods were equally grasping: this was the feeling in the palace. And there was now, in his own heart, a desperate need for a god who would be loving, helpful, understanding and kind.

Prompted by a fanaticism born of illness, he determined that this god of his could not live comfortably with the other gods — even if Amon would permit it, which he obviously would not. So all others must be swept away and be replaced by the solar disk, the essence of the sun, with its grotesque skinny arms and its grotesque tiny hands reaching down to give blessings to its lonely, grotesque son.

The sun, of course, had always been the basis of, and dominant factor, in Egyptian religion, but it was the sun as Ra-Atum in his rising, as Ra-Herakhte in his going-down, as Amon-Ra in his form combined with the greatest god, whose priests came to dominate all the others. The sun as the Aten was pure and serene and always the same — *and without the difficult problem of an established, multitudinous and power-grasping priesthood*. The Aten was pristine and perfect, waiting to be worshipped and given *his own* priesthood that would be free of the machinations of all others. He was ready-made for a mind such as the unique and absolute one that now elevated him to an absolute and unique position.

At fifteen, the boy was made co-regent with his father, amiable and ailing, and sometime in the five years of the co-regency, after his marriage to his cousin Nefertiti, he took his first long steps on the road to Amarna. He changed his name from Amonhotep IV to Akhenaten, he changed the name of Thebes from City of Amon to City of Aten, he built his temple to Aten in the Karnak precincts and established other, smaller temples to him in Nubia and Upper Egypt and probably Lower as well; and finally, when his father died, he received the blazing inspiration that became the city of Akhet-Aten, "Horizon of the Aten," and the final banishment of all the other gods.

For twelve years he reigned in Akhetaten while the empire fell away, hated Amon and other gods were driven out — and his people watched in bafflement, dismay, but never belief. His was an inward-turning religion, an exclusive and jealous worship confining to himself and Nefertiti *alone* the understanding and love of the Aten. His daughters and Tut followed him from childish duty, his courtiers followed him because some were afraid, the loyalty of others he bought with constant gifts of gold, as depicted in the Amarna tombs; but never did his religion gain any kind of hold upon the commonalty. It was indeed a "revolution," so violent that it affronted everything in all of Egypt's ancient history, by then two thousand years old; but it was revolution whose acceptance and support were confined to the palace and the court, and there in actuality only to Pharaoh and his immediate family.

Yet out of his vision of the Aten came his own Hymn to the Aten which, while similar in form to several of the major hymns to Amon and to Osiris, is illumined and made unique by an idea totally new in history up to his time—the concept of a Sole God conferring universal order and universal love upon man and all things that share the earth with him. It lives on in words still beautiful and moving:

You arise fair in the horizon of Heaven, O Living Aten, Beginner of Life. When you dawn in the east, you fill every land with your beauty. You are indeed comely, great, radiant and high over every land. Your rays embrace the lands to the full extent of all that you have made, for you are Ra and you attain their limits and subdue them for your beloved son Akhenaten. You are remote yet your rays are upon the earth. You are in the sight of men, yet your ways are not known.

When you set in the western horizon, the earth is in darkness after the manner of death. Men spend the night indoors with the head covered, the eye not seeing its fellow. Their possessions might be stolen, even when under their heads, and they would be unaware of it. Every lion comes forth from its lair and all snakes bite. Darkness is the only light, and the earth is silent when their Creator rests in his habitation.

The earth brightens when you arise in the eastern horizon and shine forth as Aten in the daytime. You drive away the night when you give forth your beams. The Two Lands are in festival. They awake and stand upon their feet, for you have raised them up. They wash their limbs, they put on raiment and raise their arms in adoration at your appearance. The entire earth performs its labors. All cattle are at peace in their pastures. The trees and herbage grow green. The birds fly from their nests, their wings raised in praise of your spirit. All animals gambol on their feet, all the winged creation live when you have risen for them. The boats sail upstream, and likewise downstream. All ways open at your dawning. The fish in the river leap in your presence. Your rays are in the midst of the sea.

You it is who causes women to conceive and makes seed into man, who gives life to the child in the womb of its mother, who comforts him so that he cries not therein, nurse that you are, even in the womb, who gives breath to quicken all that he has made. When the child comes forth from the body on the day of his birth, then you open his mouth completely and you furnish his sustenance. When the chick in the egg chirps within the shell, you give him the breath within it to sustain him. You create for him his proper term within the egg, so that he shall break it and come forth from it to testify to his completion as he runs about on his two feet when he emerges.

How manifold are your works! They are hidden from the sight of men, O Sole God, like unto whom there is no other! You fashioned the earth according to your desire when you were alone—all men, all cattle great and small, all that are upon the earth that run upon their feet or rise up on high flying with their wings. And the lands of Syria and Kush and Egypt—you appoint every man to his place and satisfy his needs. Everyone receives his sustenance and his days are numbered. Their tongues are diverse in speech and their qualities likewise, and their color is different, for you have distinguished the nations.

You make the waters under the earth and you bring them forth as the Nile at your pleasure to sustain the people of Egypt even as you have made them live for you, O Divine Lord of them all, toiling for them, the lord of every land, shining forth for them, the Aten Disk of the daytime, great in majesty!

All distant foreign lands also, you create their life. You have placed a Nile in heaven to come forth for them and make a flood upon the mountains like the sea in order to water the fields of their villages. How excellent are your plans, O Lord of Eternity!—a Nile in the sky is your gift to the foreigners and to the beasts of their lands; but the true Nile flows from under the earth for Egypt.

Your beams nourish every field and when you shine they live and grow for you. You make the seasons in order to sustain all that you have made, the winter to cool them, the summer heat that they may taste of your quality. You have made heaven afar off that you may behold all that you have made when you were alone, appearing in your aspect of the Living Aten, rising and shining forth. You make millions of forms out of yourself, towns, villages, fields, roads, the river. All eyes behold you before them, for you are the Aten of the daytime, above all that you have created.

You are in my heart, there is no other that knows you save your son Akhenaten. You have made him wise in your designs and in your might. The world is in your hand, even as you have made them. When you have risen, they live; when you set, they die, for you are duration, beyond your mere limbs. By you, men live and their eyes look upon your beauty until you set...

Since you established the earth, you have raised them up for your son, who came forth from your limbs, the King, Living in Truth, the Lord of the Two Lands, Nefer-kheperu-Ra, the Son of Ra, Living in Truth, Lord of Diadems, Akhenaten, whose life is long; and for the Great Royal Wife, his beloved, Mistress of the Two Lands, Nefer-neferu-Aten, Nefertiti, living and flourishing forever and ever.

There speaks here a visionary mind both universal and particular, a sensitive and perceptive mentality that embraces not only its own great concept of universal love but comes right down to the minutiae of daily life such as the chick in the egg, the cattle in the fields, the birds in the air. He was extremely sensitive to nature, among other things; and all living forms were included in the love of the Sole God whom he created and to whom he gave a life that has influenced mankind through many later religions, ever since.

Here at Akhet-Aten is the repository of the Amarna experiment, to which the Gem-Aten temple at Karnak, when it is restored, may provide further footnotes and perhaps embellishment. For now, this empty plain and the tombs above in the hills to north and south are the library of Akhenaten's reign. In the never-completed tomb of Aye, the aged uncle who succeeded Tutankhamon, is the most complete text of the Hymn; in the similarly uncompleted tomb of Ramose are scenes of Pharaoh and Nefertiti worshipping the Aten, and the cartouches bearing the royal titularies which Akhenaten conferred upon the god. In other tombs—all incomplete in the general chaotic ending of Akhenaten's reign, none ever occupied, rough-hewn out of the stone, brutally hacked and disfigured in the restoration of Amon but still telling the story—is preserved most of what we know about the Amarna experiment.

It is planned, so one is told, to resume full-scale excavation at Amarna just as soon as funds will permit. When Breasted published his masterwork, *A History of Egypt*, in 1905, it was possible for him to write: "One may walk its ancient streets, where the walls of the houses are still several feet high..." Now only the so-called "Northern Palace" of Nefertiti and the "Southern Palace" of Akhenaten remain aboveground; and of them, only the low mud-brick walls mentioned by Breasted, never more then two or three feet high at any point; remarkable that they are there at all after 3,300 years, but inexorably crumbling away. Beneath the level sands contributed by this century alone must lie many, many remains of other buildings, many, many artifacts, innumerable companions to the few authenticated scarabs, blue faience amulets and glassware that have found their way to the bazaar of Khan el-Khalili and the Museum in Cairo. Eventually, if the money becomes available, we may know much more about the day-to-day physical aspects of Akhet-Aten. The outlines of the city Breasted knew may once again emerge from the sands. But it does not seem likely that we will ever know much more about the real nature of Akhenaten, and about his ultimate fate and that of Nefertiti, than we do right now.

He ruled for twelve years, then vanished, as did she. A couple of years prior to his death he summarily dismissed her from his throne, placed beside him his younger brother Smenkhara as co-regent, gave to Smenkhara Nefertiti's feminine titles, had the two of them sculpted in poses of intimacy that exceed the brotherly. (He prided himself on "Living in Truth," which he affixed always to his titularies. His family life with Nefertiti and their daughters had always been exposed to the public in a way no other pharaoh before or since ever permitted. With a fanatic honesty he did the same with Smenkhara.)

Nefertiti and several of her daughters retired to the North Palace, where the child Tut also spent some time with her in her banishment. Smenkhara made some feeble attempt to act as liaison with Thebes for his brother, sinking ever deeper into physical weakness and mental despair as it became apparent that his people would have none of Aten. Then suddenly—in some cataclysmic finale precipitated by Horemheb and the underground priesthood of Amon—Akhenaten, Smenkhara, Nefertiti, the girls, all disappear, their mummies never found, with the possible exception of Smenkhara. Only nine-year-old Tut and one of the daughters, his niece Ankh-e-sen-pa-aten, whom he marries, remain; and the court returns to Thebes. Amon and the gods are restored, the chisels and battering rams go to work on Akhenaten's city and all his temples and monuments throughout the Two Lands, and it is all over.

But the unique vision of a Sole God of love and universal compassion remains and ultimately takes root elsewhere; and the position of the monarchy, although all is restored outwardly just as it was, and though such strong rulers as Horemheb, Seti I and Ramesses II wield their powers with absolute authority and conviction as before, is somehow never quite the same again. Nor is Amon, determined never again to be displaced and spurred to make sure of this by a steadily increasing thirst for power that eventually makes puppets of pharaohs and brings Hrihor the High Priest to the throne. Nor does the empire ever recover from the disintegration caused by its virtual abandonment while Akhenaten devoted himself to the single-minded worship of his god.

In an old flatbed truck that seemed barely able to navigate, we were bounced and jolted across the plain past the deserted new village, turned north, came finally to the ridge above the city where the North Tombs, locked and guarded, stand. We entered, looked them over, saw the hacked and battered remnants of the great experiment on the walls, emerged again to stand for a few moments looking south over the barren, heat-locked plain. He must have come here many times to brood over the great city at his feet, bright with banners and gold-tipped temples and obelisks and all the busy life of many, many thousands. Again the echoes rise, the ghostly hum of a great city, the tragic sighs of puzzlement of a pharaoh who could not understand why his people could not understand him when all he wanted was to preach love. For a second a strange ungainly figure rich in its royal regalia looked sidelong from slanted, narrow eyes, its long face with heavy jowl and pendulous lips alive with some anguished question, some desperate need for reassurance and explanation. Then it was gone, as fugitive as the little dust devils that whirled for an instant here and there on the valley floor and then subsided in the furnace-hot, quick-dying breeze.

For a few moments no one spoke. Silence held the plain of Akhet-Aten. Then we turned and climbed down the rocky path to the waiting truck, stopped again at the rest house, crossed the river and an hour later were back in the rush of modern Minya.

All that remains on the vast empty plain of Akhenaten's revolutionary capital, which he christened Akhet-Aten, are a few mud-brick walls representing two of the royal palaces. This, known as Nefertiti's North Palace, was where history's most beautiful queen was banished by her strange visionary husband when he chose to place beside him on the throne his younger brother Smenkhara. Here his youngest brother Tutankhamon played as a child and absorbed the Aten heresy which was ultimately to cost him his own life at the hands of vengeful Amon.

At Tuna el-Gebal, across the Nile near the western limits of Akhenaten's city, was the center of the worship of the god Thoth, that amiable soul who presided over scribes and wisdom in his two forms of the ibis and the ape. This beautifully preserved small temple and a number of mummified apes testify to his once-active priesthood. But it is not for this that most visitors come to Tuna el-Gebal. It is rather the huge stone stela, or marker, that stands in desolate isolation half a mile away ...

That night we went out and wandered through the main shopping streets, brightly lighted, filled with activity, the shops humming with life, a steady parade of men, women, children, soldiers, dogs, donkeys, horses, bicycles, autos—the evening shopping and the evening promenade, that surge of sheer fascinating life that fills all the streets and bazaars from North Africa on east through India to Hong Kong. Akhenaten, Nefertiti and Amarna seemed very far away for a while. But next day they came back.

When he established Akhet-Aten, it was not only the plain of the city itself on the east bank, but an agricultural area on the west bank to support it, as well. East-west from cliff to cliff across the river, Akhet-Aten varied from twelve to seventeen and a half miles in width. From north to south he measured it to be approximately eight miles. He marked the lot with fourteen stelae, some as high as twenty-six feet. Of these the one at Tuna el-Gebal is the one best known to visitors, and in its sad, sad loneliness perhaps the most moving of them all.

Again we drove south some twenty-five miles, turning this time to the right, away from the river, along many canals, between many fields of sugarcane, toward the western cliffs, here very low. Half an hour of this, and abruptly all cultivation and vegetation ceased. We crossed the usual knife-line that separates the Black Land from the Red and were instantly into desert. We made a long curve to the west and south, the road barely more than a dirt track over the sand. Very few people ever come here, and today there were no others. We stopped. On our right, up a long slope, nestled into the cliff, perhaps five hundred yards away, stood the boundary stela of the city of Akhet-Aten.

We walked slowly up the slope, came to it, stopped. It is perhaps fifteen feet high. It has been partially defaced, but not much. Perhaps Horemheb felt contemptuously that it was not worth the bother, it was so out of the way no one would ever see it again anyway. It shows Akhenaten, Nefertiti and two of their daughters making offerings to the Aten. Around their figures and his runs much hieroglyphic text, worn by time but much still legible.

Directly beneath his figure on the sand was the dried-out husk of a huge black beetle: god Kheperu, part of his own name, had died, by some unbelievable coincidence, at his feet. The only sound in all the stillness was the shrill squeaking of bats who inhabit the great bulge of rock that overhangs the stela to the right. All else was silence. Mighty are the words that greet the visitor:

"Year 6 [of his reign], fourth month of the second season, thirteenth day.

"Live the Good God, satisfied with truth, lord of heaven, lord of Aten; live the great one who illuminates the Two Lands; live my father; live Harakhte-Rejoicing-in-the-Horizon, in his name; 'Heat-which-is-in-Aten,' who is given life forever and ever.

"Living Horus; Mighty Bull; Beloved of Aten; Favorite of the Two Goddesses of Upper and Lower Egypt; Great in Kingship in Aten; Golden Horus; Bearer of the Name of Aten; King of Upper and Lower Egypt, Living in Truth; Lord of the Two

Akhenaten caused to be built, and personally dedicated, fourteen stelae to mark the boundaries of his city. This, one of the loneliest but also one of the most accessible, is the most frequently visited by those who come to marvel at the story of "history's first individualist."

Mighty are the words which accompany the depiction of Akhenaten, Nefertiti, and two of their six daughters receiving the blessings of the Aten. His dedication of his city to his god, he says, "shall not be erased, it shall not be washed out, it shall not be abraded, it shall not be encumbered with detritus, it shall not be destroyed. If it should disappear, if it should ever wear away, if the stela upon which it is should fall, I will restore it again anew in this place where it is ... Akhet-Aten, mountain to mountain from its eastern horizon to its western horizon, it shall belong to my father Aten, given life forever and ever." Now only the bats squeaking in the neighboring rocks break the utter silence of the desert and provide company for tragic Akhenaten and his lovely wife.

Lands; Nefer-Kheperu-Ra, Son of Ra, Living in Truth, Lord of Diadems: Akhenaten, great in duration, given life forever and ever; Good God, whose beauty Aten created, the really good-hearted toward him that made him, satisfying him with that which pleases his ka, doing that which is useful for him that begat him; offering the earth to him that placed him upon his throne, supplying his eternal house with millions and hundred thousands of things, exalter of Aten, magnifier of his name; who causes that the earth should belong to him that made him; Akhenaten.

"Hereditary princess, great in the palace, lovely of face, beautiful in the double plume, lady of joy, abounding in favor, at the sound of whose voice there is rejoicing; the Great King's Wife, his beloved, the Mistress of the Two Lands, Nefer-neferu-Aten Nefertiti..."

There follows a description of Akhenaten's decision to build the city and of his tribute to his god, and a description of the various boundary stelae and a promise that each will be maintained:

"It shall not be erased, it shall not be washed out, it shall not be abraded, it shall not be encumbered with detritus, it shall not be destroyed. If it should disappear, if it should ever wear away, if the stela upon which it is should fall, I will restore it again anew in this place where it is...

"Now, as for the width of Akhet-Aten, mountain to mountain from its eastern horizon to its western horizon, it shall belong to my father, Aten, given life forever and ever; whether it be its mountains or its cliffs, its valleys or its hills, or all its people, or all its cattle, or anything which Aten causes to exist, upon which his rays shine, or anything else of Akhet-Aten, they shall belong to my father, the living Aten, for the temple of Aten in Akhet-Aten, forever and ever..."

Here he stood 3,300 years ago, surveying what his sculptors had wrought for him on behalf of his father Aten; and here he stands still in stone, in the company of his wife and daughters. Their arms stretch up in supplication to the faceless disk which is reaching down to them with the ankh, sign of life.

And here the sands stretch out before him, empty, empty, empty; and at his feet lies god Kheperu, dead; and in the desolate silence, sad, so sad, only the squeaking bats keep court and company now for poor unhappy Nefer-Kheperu-Ra Akhenaten, Lord of the Two Lands, King of the North and South, Mighty Bull, Lord of Diadems, Beloved of Aten, Living in Truth forever and ever, for millions and millions of years.

More sugarcane, more cotton, more bumps, bangs, jolts, rattles; the train, reboarded, lurches on toward Cairo. Many businessmen, soldiers, students get on at Minya. A Palestinian student, well-spoken, pleasant, perhaps twenty-one or twenty-two, three years in university in Cairo, assists with directions. Three high-school-age Egyptians, earnest and intent, are slightly mixed up in their English but lively in their interest: "Your Majesty, how many people live in America?... Your Majesty, what do you think of Egypt?... Your Majesty, do you think Egyptian television should carry movies about sex?" This, in a Muslim country, puts Majesty on something of a spot, relieved when the train chugs in and Majesty can wave a cordial goodbye and climb aboard. Ahead lies the fulcrum of modern Egypt, el-Qahira, "the Triumphant," the sprawling, dirty, dusty, rushing, overcrowded, hectic, "impossible" but always vibrantly alive city from which harassed men try to govern a runaway population and a limping economy.

Off to the right north of Minya, a glimpse of the Middle Kingdom rock tombs of Beni Hassan; on the left, much farther north, the distant misty late-afternoon silhouettes of the Old Kingdom pyramids of Dashur and Meidum, rarely visited save by scholars, crumbling away, most of them nothing but sagging stone mounds now. Then past the small palm-fringed grassy remnant of what used to be the great capital of Memphis; past the Old Kingdom necropolis at Sakkara; a distant glimpse of the Great Pyramids; and then into the roiling life of Cairo, horns blaring, brakes screeching, people shouting, everybody rushing somewhere, doing something, in a haze of dust and smog and auto fumes, to the accompaniment of an endless cacophony of sound that never quite lets up even in the smallest hours of night.

In the last lingering days of what used to be the Roman Empire, long after it too had trailed away into twilight and all the great glories were over, the Two Lands were forgotten by history, sinking back into much the same state of rural disintegration in which Menes had found them 3,000 years B.C. In that period the Christian Copts lived in many places along the Nile, some of them in the tombs and temples which to this day show the discolorations of their cooking fires and the ruthless religious destruction of some of the most beautiful pharaonic paintings, reliefs and statuary. In about A.D. 640 the Arabs invaded Egypt, introducing Mohammedanism. From 900 to 1250 the country was ruled by a series of viziers of whom the most famous was Saladin, who fought the Christians in the Crusades. For more than 250 years after that the Mamelukes, the warrior class created by the Turks from the most able slaves captured in their wars, were in control.

In 1517 the Ottoman Turks conquered the country. Egypt officially remained part of the Ottoman Empire until World War I, although in practical fact the influence of Britain and France, builders and owners of the Suez Canal, was paramount. In 1882 the British took effective control of the country, though the Turkish connection lingered on until 1914, when Turkey and Britain became enemies and Britain immediately assumed complete legal control, though permitting an Egyptian, Fuad, to become king in 1922. His son Farouk succeeded in 1936 and Britain remained in de facto control until 1949, when she gave Egypt independence in the great sluffing-off of empire that followed World War II. Growing nationalism made the Egyptians increasingly restive, as did Farouk's playboy career and the corruption of his government. Army revolution brought his peaceable dismissal in 1952 and Gamal Abdel Nasser came to power. The British and French were finally ousted from the Suez in 1956 when Nasser nationalized it. The brief attempt by Britain, France and Israel to invade Egypt and recapture the canal was squelched by an alarmed and angry Dwight Eisenhower, then running as a peacemaker for re-election to his second term. Out of the necessities of presidential politics and the argument of bigger powers, Egypt finally emerged, after almost two thousand years, once more in complete control of her own destiny. Anwar el-Sadat became President after Nasser's death in 1970.

On the fifth of August, A.D. 969, when Mars was in the ascendant, the country's Fatimid conquerors laid the first stone of the city, naming it el-Qahira, "The Triumphant," in honor of the planet. It now has more than 8,000,000 people, making it the largest Arab and African city and a royal headache for all who live, visit, or try to govern in it.

It is even so a fascinating and likable place. Sidewalks and streets are always torn up; a constant scuff of dust rises everywhere. Traffic is a great game between driver and driver, and driver and pedestrian: an amazingly small number actually get killed. Traffic, in fact, is in some ways the great safety valve for Cairo's generally poor and underpaid residents. It is a marvelous release to miss somebody's fender or shinbone by one-sixteenth of an inch and then let him know at the top of your lungs what you think of his ancestry all the way back to Menes.

There are quieter areas, Gezira Island across the river, Maadi the southern suburb, aloof Heliopolis and the like, but the overall impression of Cairo is of teeming life and uncontrollable growth with which neither residents nor government can ever keep up. All Cairenes and in fact all Egyptians refer to it as "impossible." Many say they "hate" it. This does not stop the constant flood of newcomers who arrive daily from up the river or from the Delta, leaving towns and villages as far away as Abu Simbel, as close as Alexandria. Cairo is often called "Misr," as is Egypt itself, from the Arabic Misr-um-dunya, "Misr, Mother of the World" — and it is to Misr that the young and the jobless keep coming in an unstoppable tide that simply means that each day there are more and more young and more jobless in the city.

An economy still basically agricultural tries to support this and does not succeed. Prices are climbing. Industry is being encouraged by government subsidy and much assistance, but it is limited pretty much to processing agricultural products, and it is not taking hold very well. Nasser's dream of the High Dam has resulted in the addition of several hundred thousand more acres of cultivation, but it has upset the natural rhythm with which Hapi's inundation used to replenish the land and has increased the need for costly artificial fertilizers.

No sizeable oil reserves have been found — though with regularity delegations of foreign oilmen arrive, looking secretive, Texan and self-important, to confer with

Endless, flowing, ever moving, ever alive: the Nile, the Nile, always the Nile . . .

On camels, horses, and donkeys the
Bedouin of the desert drift through
Egyptian history, sometimes
accepted, sometimes despised— but
always there, over the next hill,
beyond the next sand dune...

Against a background of modern power lines, members of the desert's most ancient transportation system groan, grunt, snort and spit their supercilious way through a tough, painful and unrelievedly harsh and cruel life.

the President—and the promise that they will be found so far remains a will-o'-the-wisp. The country is heavily in debt to its increasingly hostile Arab neighbors, principally Saudi Arabia, and to everyone else who will lend it money. An attempt to raise bread prices in 1977 brought street rioting and a prompt backdown by the government. There are rumors of much corruption at high levels, and there is much unrest, potentially explosive, among the poor. Yet Sadat is enormously popular. His people genuinely and desperately want peace with Israel because they want no more sons killed and they are convinced that a genuine trading partnership with the Israelis would give them economic security and great international influence. But in actual fact Egypt at the moment is one of the principal "sick men" of the Middle East, with no easy cure—perhap no lasting cure at all, if one is really practical—in sight in the foreseeable future.

Overlying this is a thin stratum of the rich, who control the major elements of the economy, winter in Europe or the States, escape the suffocating heat of high summer by going to villas along the shore around Alexandria, drive beautiful cars, live in beautiful homes, and observe, with that patient superiority which characterizes the very rich everywhere, the unfortunate goings-on below. Also like the very rich everywhere, they are prepared to take flight at any moment if they have to. Swiss bank accounts and discreet investments abroad hedge many a well-to-do home in Cairo and "Alex." A genuine but somehow detached and disinterested concern infuses the attitude toward the fellahin in the fields and the jobless in the streets. All that is quite disturbing and frustrating, but at least *we*, in *our* snug houses, are taken care of.

Thus it has ever been in the Two Lands: Pharaoh, his generals and the nobility live in luxury, and the peasants live far below. But there are of course several very sharp differences. There is no pharaonic tradition to hold it all together, although Sadat has a genuine fatherly concern for his people, particularly in the villages from which he came; and while there is a dominant religion, it is not sufficiently strong to fill the void — though in a repressive sense, it makes the attempt.

The government, prompted by Muslim leaders who exercise a considerable behind-the-scenes influence, recently inaugurated a campaign to "restore discipline to the streets of Cairo," cracking down on a range of offenders from beggars to traffic violators (a challenge there for a pharaoh, that one suspects not even Horemheb or Ramesses II could handle) to those who are guilty of "obscene conduct" in public. In a Muslim country this can be something as innocent as kissing your girl in public. "Thousands" of uniformed and plainclothes policemen have been mobilized, so we are told, to do all this. One imagines how far they are succeeding with the basically religious—but not *that* religious—Cairenes.

Egypt appears to be too easygoing for that sort of thing, its people too independent. Of all the Arab peoples, they seem least likely to bow to anything smacking of religious fanaticism. Yet it could happen under the right circumstances, of course: no one should confidently predict the stability of any Arab country. But as long as the present government lasts, the chances are against it. Sadat's rule is a curious combination of semi-dictatorship and semi-freedom, so inextricably intermingled that its subtleties elude the observer: all one can say is that "it will last, inshallah." The visitor hopes devoutly that it will, because Egypt, desperately beset by problems though she may be, is still the best and most encouraging hope that there can ultimately be some reasonable stability in that hectic corner of the world...

Entertained, wined, dined, relaxing a bit as the journey begins to wind down, one can forget all this for a little while in the all-embracing warmth of Egyptian hospitality. Thanks to the kindness and generosity of very likable Yusef Gaafar, owner of Eastmar Travel, and his equally likable assistant, Hesham Imam, various things were made easy. The most interesting was a trip to Alexandria through the Delta, where the richest land in Egypt covers the palaces, tombs, temples, homes, relics of the Old Kingdom, most of which will probably never be found now, so deeply do they lie buried beneath five millennia of Hapi's flooding.

Alexandria, thanks to Lawrence Durrell, is a rosily romantic dream to most who have read his novels. If it ever was that romantic, it is not now. There is, it is true, a certain leisurely pace that Cairo with its millions can never match: there just aren't that many people. The streets are broader, the squares and parks more numerous, the autos fewer—it is just a smaller city, and it is also one that has always been oriented more toward the western Mediterranean than toward the east. Somewhere beneath its aging and dilapidated remnants of charm lie the bones of the Macedonian. Alexander was brought back here from his death in Babylon to be interred with full pharaonic rites. It seems impossible that his tomb will ever be found, but someday, somehow, in some modern excavation or unexpected disturbance of the earth, it still could be. It would be the greatest sensation since the discovery of Tutankhamon. Like Tut, he would not be surprised by this.

The Alexandria waterfront, that famed corniche which may once, in its heyday as a playground for Europe's wealthy, have been a gracious and beautiful promenade, is now a cluster of rundown apartment houses and dying hotels. It is much cooler there, and in summer when Cairo is broiling many who can afford it escape to the beaches east and west of the city, there to relax in private villas along the sand. Its restaurants, concentrating naturally enough on seafood, are adequate; and the food is fresh.

Its antiquities are Greek and Roman, its ties to ancient Egypt of course extremely tenuous. Its ties to Cairo and the rest of Egypt seem equally so. Cairenes look down on Alexandria, Alexandrians on Cairo. Alexandria is a sport, an offside child, which sits out on the Mediterranean shore both physically and psychologically distant from the capital and the 700-mile life of the valley of the Nile. The President, who has a rest house in Aswan, will presently be spending some of his summer days in Farouk's former palace east of the city, which is being remodeled and refurbished for his use. But the heart of Egypt does not beat in Alexandria. It lies elsewhere, closer to the old roots.

We drove back on the southern road, straight across the desert toward the low distant hills guarding the west bank of the Nile at Cairo. We met few cars, some camels; saw in the distance from time to time interesting-looking mounds, remnants of very ancient pyramids, undisturbed as yet but no doubt on somebody's list for exploration—some day—"when money permits."

Presently the empty desolation of the desert began to give way to vegetation. We turned and twisted along a low pass through the hills. City lights began to increase, traffic increased, people increased. We entered paved and lighted streets, the familiar cacophony, the familiar rush. In the rapidly gathering dusk the lighted pyramids of Giza welcomed us back.

Founded by Alexander the Great, made famous by romantic novelists and by fashionable European visitors long since gone to rest, Alexandria is possessed of fresh seafood restaurants, a shabby waterfront and the remnants of an aging and dilapidated charm.

T hey do not appear so large when one first sees them from the highway running west out of Cairo; but as one gets nearer they begin to grow in size, so that when the car finally comes to a halt amid the bead-sellers, the volunteer "guides" and the groaning, supercilious camels, they loom above ponderous, gigantic, having on the mind exactly the effect their builders intended them to have when they were constructed nearly five thousand years ago. They were meant to astound and overwhelm and they do. Whether, as some hold, they were also meant to house great mathematical secrets conferred by visitors from outer space or Atlantis is another matter. The theories are fun and they require considerable imagination and a lot of mental gymnastics. One wonders what those whom the Greeks called Cheops, Chephren, and Mycerinas — and the Egyptians Khufu, Khafra and Men-kur-Ra — would have made of them.

They wanted to be absolutely sure they weren't forgotten, and in this they succeeded beyond the wildest dreams of all men but themselves, who were, like many pharaohs, far out on the edge where humanity, divinity and reality got just a trifle mixed up in the pharaonic mind.

In any event, there they stand: the "Great Pyramid" of Cheops, the somewhat lesser pyramid of his presumed son Chephren, and the much smaller pyramid of Chephren's successor Mycerinas. The last two contain sufficient records on the walls so that their builders are established beyond reasonable doubt. They are considerably less sophisticated than the Great Pyramid of Cheops which stands alongside them. Indeed, nobody really knows for sure that Cheops really built the Great Pyramid. What has been interpreted to be his name is painted on a single ceiling block in one of the interior chambers; otherwise, there is no solid evidence linking him to the Great Pyramid. There it stands, quite unique. From that point, the "pyramidologists" take off.

Before they do, however, the workaday statistics are impressive enough.

Khufu's Great Pyramid erected somewhere around 2690 B.C. in the Fourth Dynasty: original height approximately 481 feet, now slightly less since the capstone, probably of alabaster, was pilfered millennia ago for other buildings by other pharaohs; estimated to contain somewhere between 2,300,000 and 2,500,000 blocks of limestone, of an average weight of two and a half tons each, joined to a fineness of one fiftieth of an inch and sealed with a cement so tenacious that blocks cannot be separated without cracking; a square base, almost mathematically exact, of 755 feet to a side, comprising an area which various people have played with over the years, some estimating that it could encompass St. Peter's, St. Paul's, Westminster Abbey and the cathedrals of Florence and Milan at the same time — and Napoleon, using his intuition, saying that the cubic content is enough to encircle France completely with a wall ten feet high and a foot thick. Its construction took, according to Herodotus' curbstone guess, twenty years, with a hundred thousand men working each year during the three-month inundation.

Dirty, dusty, overcrowded, "impossible," yet always vibrant and alive, Cairo is favored by romantic haze and its nearness to the pyramids of Giza.

The pyramids at Giza honor the monumental egos of three of the earliest pharaohs—Cheops, Chephren, and Mycerinas. In any light, at any time, they are overwhelmingly impressive—perhaps mostly so at dawn and dusk. In recent years mathematicians and imaginative scientists have tried to make much of their sittings, heights, and angles, projecting therefrom theories that reach as far as Atlantis and outer space. Probably such mental gymnastics are unnecessary. The pyramids make their own statement—of great power, wielded by absolute rulers who were determined to make of their final statements on earth objects so vast and monumental that they would forever humble future generations. And so they have.

Alongside the Great Pyramid at Giza, a jumble of smaller pyramids marks the final resting-places of pharaohs and their queens.

Khafra's pyramid, built somewhere around 2650 B.C.: approximately 450 feet in height; other characteristics not so unique or mulled-over; dismissed as No. 2 while controversies swirl around No. 1.

And finally *Menkura's*, erected about 2600 B.C.; only 190 feet in height: a relatively minor No. 3 on the plateau of Giza overlooking Cairo, though, seen with the other two, partner in a most impressive triad; and itself nothing to be sneezed at, or anything that would fit easily into the average back yard.

Then there are the Great Pyramid statistics that conjure up so many mental gymnastics because they are, quite simply, unexplainable in terms of the rather simple, rather limited, rather primitive people whom the visitor meets when entering the realm of Ancient Egypt.

Each side of the pyramid faces one of the cardinal points of the compass, an orientation so accurate that a compass can be checked for error against it ... a positioning so exact that it is out of alignment with true north by only four minutes of arc ... a maximum deviation from a perfect right angle in the square of the base of no more than one twentieth of a degree.

Add the mathematical games: take the length of one side of the pyramid and divide it by one half the height, and one arrives at *pi*, 3.14159, accurate to five decimal points, *pi* being the geometric relation of the diameter of a circle to its circumference — this from a people who had a serviceable but crude system of mathematics (14 would be written 10 plus 1 plus 1 plus 1 plus 1, for instance) a modest knowledge of astronomy, and the first calendar of 365 days — but otherwise left no evidence of any outstanding mathematical or geometric accomplishment.

The pyramids, too, have their protectors. The fences are a little rickety but the guards will let you in if you can produce sufficient baksheesh.

And the games go further: using a "pyramid inch" slightly longer than our own (thus perhaps stacking the deck a bit, but all in a spirit of good clean pyramidal fun), the pyramidologists arrive at the conclusion that the builders knew the world was round, and also knew its approximate size. Further than that, they use the angles at the points where internal passages and chambers intersect to extrapolate from them a drawing that demonstrates the geometry of the circle. And by combining "pyramid inches" and a time scale, they arbitrarily wrench the passages and chambers into a complicated chronology which is supposed to have prophesied every major event from the Crucifixion to World War I.

Add to this "pyramid power," which is supposed to sharpen razor blades, preserve dead fish and revive stale vegetables, and you have quite an absorbing puzzle with which to while away the time.

What Thoth and Osiris and Horus and Hathor, to say nothing of Tuthmose III, Hatshepsut, Akhenaten, Tut and Ramesses II, would have made of all this, one can only imagine. It is usually enough for the visitor to see the things; as, one suspects, it was enough for Khufu, Khafra and Menkura to have them built. Khufu in particular must have felt that his Great Pyramid was a mighty fine tomb, the biggest in history and perfectly suited to his glory as a god-king. And so it is. And so are they all.

Approaching the group at the best hours, early morning or late afternoon, the visitor can feel something of the primordial awe with which the Ancients viewed it throughout their long history. The pyramids were already more than 1,000 years old when the Eighteenth Dynasty came to power; objects of superstitious veneration but also, probably, of simple tourist wonderment, as they are for us. There isn't any great necessity to explain them in far-out, esoteric ways. They make their own statement.

Napoleon spent a night in the Great Pyramid and emerged shaken from some experience he never divulged to the end of his days. There have been some others over the millennia who have done the same, with the same result. Even in broad daylight, to crawl in a back-cracking half stoop down the long slanting passageways to the so-called "Queen's Chamber" and the rough-hewn room wherein rests a large stone trough that presumably housed Khufu's sarcophagus, is to feel a combination of physical discomfort and mental oppression that commands both respect and a certain superstitious awe. It is not the geometric games that really impress, at the pyramids; it is simply the massive physical statement of *power*, the dead weight of very great age, and the infinite and disturbing sense of time running endlessly backward into the remotest mists of unknowable antiquity.

Some five hundred feet southeast of the Great Pyramid, facing east to greet Ra in the morning, reclines Har-makh-is the Sphinx, bearing an enigmatic expression, damaged, but perhaps made thereby even more susceptible to fanciful imaginings, by the gun practice of Turkish conquerors. The face is presumed to be that of Khafra. The sphinx-form is standard throughout much of Ancient Egyptian sculpture, used to associate pharaohs (and sometimes queens) with the strength and conquering qualities of the lion.

An unassailable dignity surrounds the Sphinx. It is possible to anthropomorphize Harmakhis very easily: surely there must be secrets behind that worn, patient, indomitable face. It is no wonder everyone from the earliest pharaohs on down through Caesar, Augustus, Napoleon and you and me has tried to imagine them and been frustrated yet fascinated by their imperturbable inaccessibility.

Harmakhis has lived very long and seen very many things; and with him we return to our verbose and boastful friends in the Great House, and, in particular, to Tuthmose IV.

"When His Majesty was a youth like Horus... he did a thing that gave him pleasure on the highlands of the Memphis nome, upon its southern and northern road, shooting at a target with copper bolts, hunting lions and wild goats, racing in his chariot, his horses swifter than the wind, together with two companions, while not a soul knew it.

"When the time came for him to rest his followers, it was in the usual place at the side of Harmakhis... the splendid place of the beginning of time..."

Harmakhis had his troubles. In the thousand years since his sculpting under Khafra, he had become considerably neglected and the sands in consequence had

Against the sunset the ruins of
Giza make their statement, ancient
and mysterious.

"At the side of Harmakhis . . .
the splendid place of the
beginning of time." *So wrote
Tuthmose IV of the Sphinx of Giza,
and so Harmakhis the Sphinx seems
to the visitor to this very day—the
crowning monument of a splendid
place at the beginning of time. His
face damaged by the gun practice of
Turkish occupiers centuries ago, he
sits with a somber and unassailable
dignity at the foot of the pyramids,
seeming to contain the secrets of
untold ages and ancient, far-off
things. Pharaohs, kings and
commoners from around the world
have come to ponder him, and none
has gone away satisfied that he
knows what Harmakhis is thinking.
But very few go away really
convinced that he is simply cold
stone and is not thinking: the
impact of Harmakhis is far too
powerful for that.*

piled around him. On one of his hunting days, young Tuthmose fell asleep in his shadow and in his dream Harmakhis spoke "with his own mouth, as a father speaks with his son, saying:

"'Behold me! See me, Tuthmose! I am your father, Harmakhis-Kheperu-Ra-Atum, who will give you my kingdom on earth at the head of the living. You will wear the white crown and the red crown... The land shall be yours in its length and breadth... The food of the Two Lands shall be yours, the great tribute of all countries, for a long time. My face is yours, my desire is toward you. You will be a protector to me, because I feel as though I were failing in all my limbs. The sand of this desert upon which I am has reached me. Turn to me, have that done which I desire, knowing that you are my son, my protector...'"

Tuthmose relates that when he awoke he understood Harmakhis' cry for help, muffled by the encroaching sands, and made up his mind that if Harmakhis kept his part of the bargain and made him Pharaoh, he would keep his and clear away the sand. In due course both events occurred, and since that time, with some occasional lapses, Harmakhis has been kept free from the drifts and allowed to appear as impressive as he is.

From Sphinx to smaller sphinx, one proceeds to all that is left of Memphis, some eleven miles farther on south and west of Cairo, Menes' capital at the start of the First Dynasty and often subsequently the residence of the kings when for one reason or another they did not wish to rule from Thebes. According to the gossip Herodotus picked up in his late time, Menes built a great wall to divert the course of the Nile around his city. Because he wore the white crown of Upper Egypt, this was known as the "White Wall" after his residence in Upper Egypt, which had been known as the "White House" (a name carried on down later to designate Pharaoh's treasury). His residence in Memphis became the "Great House," and it is as the "Great House" that Pharaoh's palace was generally known thereafter. From this name, in fact—"Per-O" as translated by early Egyptologists—came the word "Pharaoh" itself. In time the two became interchangeable, as today one says, "The White House wants—" to mean "The President wants—" Except that there was one difference. In the Two Lands what Per-O wanted, Pharaoh generally got.

In the necropolis of Sakkara stands the "Step Pyramid" of King Zoser of the Third Dynasty, the first pharaoh to introduce building in stone on a large scale. The Step Pyramid, so-called because it is constructed in a series of six steplike diminishing levels reaching a height of 195 feet, was built under the direction of a remarkable scribe-architect-counselor known as Im-ho-tep, a man reputedly of such wisdom that he became in later dynasties the patron saint of scribes and was deified 2,500 years later as a god of medicine. Zoser's somber-eyed statue in the Cairo Museum suggests a king of profound passions and implacable force, who greatly increased the wealth and power of the Third Dynasty. His pyramid is massive and impressive because of its age, but the workmanship is primitive compared to the Giza three. It has inspired no intriguing theories of spacemen or Atlanteans.

Arrived at the main staging area for the visit to Sakkara, one finds once more horse carriages, bickering drivers, the necessity to strike a hard bargain in advance before one is rattled away across the hills and bumps of the necropolis to visit the major tombs. Sakkara is a city of death constructed on a relatively level plain with none of the dramatic natural backdrops of the Theban necropolis; yet in many of its tombs or "mastabas"—the low rectangular mud-brick structures that housed the dead in the earliest dynasties—there are to be found scenes of everyday life as charming and vivid as can be found anywhere in Egypt. From the earliest times Egyptian artists seem to have been free to depict daily life as they saw it; and they saw it through eyes and hearts that thoroughly enjoyed all its human and happy aspects.

Also at Sakkara the visitor descends beneath the earth into one of the more fantastic offshoots of Egyptian mythology—the Serapeum, burial place of the sacred Apis bulls. Sixty-four of these, mummified with all the care given a pharaoh, were discovered in the Serapeum in 1851. Their echoing stone stalls are empty and eerie now; their story fits very well into the usual deft and straight-faced illogic with which the Ancients surrounded their religion.

The Apis bull was a form of Hapi, and therefore, like the Nile, was a fertility god. He was also worshipped as the double or deputy of the God Ptah. In another layer of priestly accretions he also became known as the incarnation of a son of Osiris and as the "life of Osiris"—the name Osiris-Apis presently evolving into Serapis. He was also known as a heaven god, or, conversely, as an underworld god. He was also associated with Atum and the various gods, including Khonsu of Thebes, who represented the moon. Quite a load for one dumb, and no doubt at times rather puzzled, animal to bear. The one selected led a strange and colorful life.

He was believed to have been conceived by a ray of light descending upon a cow incapable of bearing a calf, and he was elected by a special priest who was appointed to travel up and down the Two Lands until he found him. There were twenty-nine distinguishing marks, including that he must be black, must have a triangular white patch on his forehead, a patch resembling an eagle on his back, double hairs in his tail, and the form of a scarab on his tongue. Herodotus heard that everybody in the country rejoiced and put on bright clothing when he was discovered: another excuse for a party, apparently.

His discovery meant bad news for his predecessor, presumably old anyway but still enjoying his pleasant life in the sacred stable at Memphis, switching his tail to knock off the flies and placidly munching on the bountiful grain placed before him by reverent priests. As soon as the new Apis was discovered the old one's happy life came to an abrupt end via ceremonial drowning in the Nile. His flesh was eaten by the priests, but his skin, bones and other parts were mummified. He was given full royal funerary rites, including sixty days of public mourning (compared with seventy for a pharaoh), was provided with human *ushabti* to take care of him in the afterworld, and was buried with great ceremony at Sakkara. The Serapeum was begun in the Eighteenth Dynasty and in it the significant life dates of all the buried bulls were faithfully recorded. Even Akhenaten, with some inconsistency, did not disturb the worship of the Apis bulls.

It was a nice life while it lasted. The bull was kept in a court near the southern gate of the sanctuary of Ptah at Memphis; was placed on a throne from time to time and honored with festivals; and his advice was sought on many matters, which he presumedly decided with a shake of his head, a flick of the tail, or, depending on the gravity of the question, a bellow.

Under Ptolemy Soter, some time around 200 B.C., the center of Apis' cult was moved from Memphis to Alexandria. Ptolemy built a new Serapeum there (Sakkara, like Karnak, having centuries ago sunk beneath the sands) and from that point the Apis cult spread to Athens and other parts of the Greek Empire, and from there to Rome, where it lasted for several centuries.

Archeological exploration continues steadily at Sakkara, a vast storehouse of the Old Kingdom. Two tombs of Horemheb have been found, one, now destroyed, described by Breasted and another discovered within the past three years. Neither was occupied, nor has one ever been found in the Valley of the Kings; ironically, the body of the destroyer of Akhenaten and Nefertiti seems to be as homeless as theirs.

Looking out over the enormous plain of Sakkara from the elevated point where one arrives, one realizes how much still lies beneath the sands of Egypt and how much there is yet to learn about the very human and very likable people of the Two Lands. The Cairo Museum, that dusty over-crammed jumble of their glories, is the suitable place from which to bid them all goodbye.

On a plain even more ancient than Giza, the crumbling pyramids of the earliest pharaohs dominate the skyline at Sakkara.

Beneath Sakkara's sands lie
Egypt's oldest tombs, above, her
oldest pyramids. Archeologists may
dig for centuries and still not
discover all that Sakkara holds.

The building is massive, squat, made of brown limestone, separated by a lawn filled with statues, stelae and miscellaneous pharaonic heads from the chaotic dust and confusion caused by nearby hotel construction and the unending clamor of Cairo traffic. Outwardly it is not so very impressive, but inside is all of Ancient Egypt—not as neatly or cleanly organized as one would like, certainly not as much so as the Egyptians themselves would like, but with the promise of better things to come. Much of the money from Tut's exhibit will be used for the construction of a wing devoted exclusively to the contents of his tomb. The old museum will be reorganized, cleaned of its endless dust, its exhibits pared to their essentials—fifty of the finest representative *ushabtis*, say, rather than 1,500 of all grades and conditions, strewn helter-skelter throughout the museum; and so on.

It is hoped that the end result may be, though on a much grander scale, as direct, clean-cut, beautifully lighted and beautifully presented as the Luxor Museum already is. Something of the old museum's rather charming chaos will be lost; but the gain in clarity and forcefulness and presentation will bring it to its full potential as perhaps the world's most fascinating record of a single people through all the stages of their national life.

For here they all are, king, queen, scribe, priest, noble, official, commoner, herdsman, soldier, slave, oarsman, vintner, housewife, child, with all their tools, plows, animals and household goods, their crowns, jewels, rods, scepters, their chariots, scarabs and sarcophagi, their turquoise, carnelian, faience and gold. Here they stand, sit, work, recline, hunt, walk, race, leap, just as they were sculpted or painted millennia ago; busy at their tasks if they be commoners, staring out with impassive smiles upon the visitor if they be royalty or nobles, serene and unchanging as they wished themselves to appear forever and ever, for millions and millions of years.

From all over the Two Lands they have been gathered, harvest of the sometimes scientific, sometimes avaricious searchings of their own people and of foreigners, brought under a single roof to attest to the life they had and the Two Lands they lived in.

If the visitor follows the suggestion of the museum guidebook, which is the most logical and interesting way to proceed, one moves in easy progression from the pre-dynastic period to the earliest dynasties of the Old Kingdom, on down through the Middle Kingdom, the Empire, Akhenaten, Tutankhamon and the later dynasties. Some hated one another; some plundered one another's monuments; some despised and vilified one another's memories.

They are all here together now.

It is here, if one follows the journey we took, that one pays one's last respects to Hatshepsut, smiling blandly from a dozen statues; to Akhenaten, colossal, gaunt and strange, standing in his special room surrounded by the smaller statues of Nefertiti, their daughters, and the jewelry and artifacts of Amarna; to Amonhotep III and

Tiye, smiling placidly, arms entwined, from their colossal statues in the main hall; to all the "wonderful things" that were buried with Tut; to the final statues of Ramesses II and many other Ramessids; to Seti I and Zoser and the Apis bull; to Amon, Ptah, Horus, Thoth and all the other gods; and, finally, in the Mummy Room, an eerie, dramatic, and—remembering what one has seen of what they were and what they did—moving farewell to the actual men themselves.

Here *is* Ramesses II. Here *is* Seti I. Here *is* Amonhotep III, "the Magnificent"—and Ahmose I, founder of the Eighteenth Dynasty—and Tuthmose III, creator of the Empire—and Merneptah, who may or not have been the pharaoh of the Exodus (no slightest trace of the alleged presence of the Israelites in Egypt has ever been found in any Egyptian records)—and horribly battered Sekenenra III of the Seventeenth Dynasty, killed fighting the Hyksos—and the enormous distended skull which is all that remains of unhappy Smenkhara, dead with Akhenaten in the lost experiment of Amarna. And many more, several of them Ramessids, some of them queens; here, mummified, the actual flesh, the Good Gods of the Great House, in person.

Most of them were found after wanderings which began when the First Prophets of Amon of the Twenty-first Dynasty realized that most of their tombs had been plundered and that the mummies themselves would be in danger if left in the Valley of the Kings any longer. Many had been unwrapped, their crowns, jewels, scarabs, gold sarcophagi, *ushabtis*, furniture and artifacts all torn away by the robbers.

They were rewrapped, given new coffins, buried again with formal rites in several different tombs; but by the time of Sheshonk I, first king of the Twenty-second Dynasty, it was obvious that they must be moved again if the ever-diligent ancestors of the folk of el-Qurna were to be thwarted.

Those that were in bad condition were mingled with the mummies of the Twenty-first Dynasty priests of Amon who had first rescued them, and were placed in a small chamber of the tomb of Amonhotep II in the Valley of the Kings. Those in better condition were placed in an Eleventh Dynasty tomb in the rocks near Deir el-Bahri.

Peace and silence then descended upon them for three thousand years, until sometime in A.D. 1875.

At that point relics began to float into the shops of Luxor and Cairo in such quantity that the Department of Antiquities became suspicious. It still took six years of investigation and a falling-out among members of the family of the sheik of el-Qurna before the Deir el-Bahri cache was finally revealed to the authorities in 1881. It was not until seventeen years later, in 1898, that the tomb of Amonhotep II was finally officially discovered. The two hiding places yielded the remains of thirty-three kings, queens, princes, first prophets of Amon and ten nobles of secondary rank.

The mummies were taken by boat down the Nile to Cairo. Men and women of the Two Lands lined the Nile in thousands to see them pass, the women weeping and wailing and pouring dust on their heads in an eerie replay of the royal burials thirty centuries before.

In Cairo the mummies were once more unwrapped, this time with scientific care by Egyptologists and doctors who photographed them, recorded their measurements and in some cases determined how they died. Sekenenra's wounds are of course obvious, and the contorted form of a nameless prince clearly indicates poison; but only scientific study could have disclosed that Ramesses V died of smallpox. A still later study, published in 1973 under the title *X-Raying the Pharaohs*, by Dr. Kent Weeks and Dr. James Harris, was conducted by a team from the University of Michigan. It found such intriguing items as that Ahmose I, unlike most Egyptian males, was not circumcised and may have been a hemophiliac; that Queen Mery-et-Amon, sister and wife of Amonhotep I, had arthritis and scoliosis; that Ramesses II and his son Merneptah both suffered from extensive dental problems; that Sip-tah, son of Seti II, probably had polio; and that the mummy of the "elder woman" found in the tomb of Amonhotep II may possibly—just possibly—be that of Hatshepsut, since her left hand is placed over the chest "in the position observed in many pharaohs after Tuthmose I." (Of such slender strands are the excitements of the science of Egyptology.)

There they lie, each in his or her hermetically sealed, humidity-proofed glass case, many with hair and teeth intact, features still clearly defined. Some dyed their hair with henna: the reddish tinge is still there, after so infinitely long a time. Those who were weak look weak. Those who were strong look strong. Seti I was a handsome man 3,100 years ago: he is, if somewhat leathery, handsome still. There they lie, some of the greatest rulers of the Two Lands, just as they were sealed away on the day they went before the forty-two judges and passed into the happy life of the afterworld. Outside roars the traffic of Cairo. Only a couple of years ago, supposedly suffering some parasite that had somehow invaded his case, one of them—and you know who—was taken briefly to France for cure. It caused a minor international sensation: Ramesses II, grabbing the headlines still.

So one leaves the Museum, leaves Cairo, leaves the Two Lands. Three millennia of history and a good-natured, hard-pressed, worried present-day people fall away below. A last glimpse of the Red Land and the Black Land, a quick swing across the lush fields of the Delta and then north over the Great Green to Europe, and home. What of the journey, and what of the smile?

Of the journey, going so far back into time, it can be said that for most who are able to make it in some leisure and with some imagination, it is one of the world's great and unforgettable experiences. It does not take much to people Karnak or the Theban necropolis or Amarna or the Nile with the still-vibrant Ancients: they demand that one allow them to come to life. Given half a chance, they do. Their presence is everywhere among their tombs and monuments, their busy existence goes on all around one; they form a ghostly yet almost palpable overlay to everything. The Two Lands confront the visitor with his own mortality, yet hold out the hope that in some fashion he, too, may achieve the immortality these amiable little people have managed to achieve; even though their immortality is based in many instances upon accident, archeological discovery and the willing worship of later generations who have made of their ruins and records one of the lasting wonders of the world.

Therefore, possibly, the smile. Despite the great recurring adversities of their history, an indomitable will held them for three thousand years to a vision of serenity, stability and peace of which the smile is the most recurrent outward symbol. They had their terrible times of turmoil, and in the First Intermediate Period someone left "The Dispute with His Soul of One Who Is Tired of Life," which in part asks bitterly:

To whom do I speak today?
Men are covetous,
Every one seizes his neighbor's goods.

To whom do I speak today?
Gentleness has perished.
Insolence has come to all men . . .

To whom do I speak today?
None remembers the past,
None at this moment does good to him who has done it . . .

To whom do I speak today?
I am laden with misery
And lack a trusty friend.

To whom do I speak today?
The sin that smites the land.
It has no end . . .

The plaint ends with a threat of suicide.

This was a commoner. Amonemhet I of the Twelfth Dynasty was by his own account and history's a good king, one who had done much for his people. He was another of the pharaohs who were almost killed in a palace conspiracy, saving his life only because he awoke suddenly and drove off his would-be assassins before they could strike him. He addressed this equally bitter abjuration to his son and co-regent, Sesostris I:

"Harden yourself against all subordinates.

"The people give heed to him who terrorizes them; approach them not alone.

"Fill not your heart with a brother, know not a friend, nor make for yourself intimates, wherein there is no end.

"When you sleep, guard for yourself your own heart, for a man has no people in the day of evil.

"I gave to the beggar, I nourished the orphan; admitted the insignificant as well as him who was great. But he who ate my food made insurrection, he to whom I gave my hand aroused fear therein.

"They who put on my fine linen looked upon me as dirt.

"They who anointed themselves with my myrrh, defiled me . . ."

Yet such bitterness is very rare in the records as we know them. The commoner who debated with his own soul was soothed at last by his soul, which urged him to "Cease lamentations, my comrade, my brother . . . I will abide here, if you reject the West [death]. But when you reach the West [in the natural course of things], and your body is united with the earth, then I will alight where you rest. Let us have an abode together." And bitter Amonemhet I lived on for several years of fruitful co-regency with his son, and the angry outrage prompted by the attack upon him gradually eased.

Not often is there bitterness in the records of the Ancients, and only in an impersonal sort of way is there hatred, even for such enemies as "wretched Kush" and "the Nine Bows," which represented the subject peoples of the empire. They are more to be pitied than censured, one gathers, having the misfortune to be so inferior to the residents of the Two Lands. It is true that from time to time some of their leaders were strung up on the prow of Pharaoh's barge, or had their hands cut off, or found themselves dangling upside down from the walls of Karnak until they died. But in the main the treatment of enemies, like the treatment of rival gods, was usually surprisingly tolerant. They were generally absorbed rather than eradicated. The Ancient Egyptians were not much for either hatred or despair, because always the memory of "the first occasion" sustained them, and the confidence that sooner or later its beneficent certainties would return.

They were not, as we have seen, a great scientific or mathematical people, nor did they have great medical expertise, though myths have been built up about all these things over the years. Nor did they have great culture in the sense of abstract, profound or philosophic art or literature, nor is there any great philosophical and political sophistication running through their history. Everything revolved around their government and around Pharaoh as its temporal-cum-spiritual head and Amon as its dominant god, which in turn conditioned and controlled their entire society. They were enormously creative in the sense that they were highly skilled builders, sculptors, painters, jewelers and goldsmiths; but always their efforts lay within the pattern. There was no encouragement—as, they felt, no reason—to venture to break out. The common, happy things of life were portrayed in a certain way; the stylized life of the pharaohs, except for Akhenaten and to some degree Tutankhamon, were portrayed in a certain way; and that was it. These things were of no interest to other lands, nor was there anything in other lands which they deemed worthy of imitation.

Therefore it can be said that in a sense, snug and smug and relatively secure for long periods behind the ramparts of their narrow, protected valley, they took from no one and they gave to no one. They were, in a way far more exclusive than most in history, sufficient unto themselves. In this they were unique then and unique now. It is why the tourist cliche has it that "there is nothing like Ancient Egypt." There really isn't.

Though usually defined indirectly, as in the "Negative Confession" of the newly dead, they did have a general sense of morality and good conduct, even though, as Breasted remarks with some tartness, "there is no doubt that side by side with these wholesome ideals of the wise and virtuous there also existed widespread and gross immorality." In this they were not much different from any other people, including our own; but as with other peoples, including our own, the sum total of the society came down on the side of decency and morality rather than indecency and immorality. With notable exceptions (much more muted and kept in proper perspective than that in our enlightened and archly all-knowing age) the average citizen was reasonably good and well behaved. His attitude toward life was tolerant, pragmatic, good-hearted and well-meaning, just as it is in Egypt today. Some of his basic precepts were best summed up in what is known to scholars as "The Instruction of Ptah-ho-tep," vizier under King Issi, next to last king of the Fifth Dynasty, written about 2400 B.C. but passed on down in the form of a school book and guide to conduct until at least the Eighteenth Dynasty. They read in part:

"Be not arrogant because you may have knowledge, and don't puff yourself up because you are a learned man. Take counsel with the ignorant as well as the wise, for the limits of art cannot be reached, and no artist completely fulfills his skill...

"Wrongdoing has never yet brought its venture to port. Evil indeed wins wealth, but the strength of truth is that it endures. The upright man says, 'It is the greatest gift my father gave me...'

"Hold fast to the truth and overstep it not, even if you thereby tell nothing that is gratifying... Be discreet in your intercourse with other people... Proclaim your business without concealment...

"If you desire your conduct to be good, to set yourself free from all that is evil, then beware of covetousness, which is a malady distasteful and incurable. Intimacy with it is impossible; it makes the sweet friend bitter, it alienates the trusted one from the master, it makes bad both father and mother, together with the brothers of the mother, and it divorces the wife. It is the sum of every kind of evil, a collection of everything that is blameworthy. Long-lived is the man whose rule of conduct is right, and who goes in accordance with the right course. He wins wealth thereby, but the covetous has no tomb [a sign of the utmost poverty]..."

These and the "instructions" of other sages were drummed into the heads of schoolboys for many centuries, and quite possibly had some effect—by osmosis, as with most schoolboys, if nothing else.

Many men stated on their tombs how well they had conducted themselves, but Pepi-Nakht of Elephantine at Aswan, scribe and counselor to King Pepi II of the Sixth Dynasty, perhaps summed up the universal ideal as well as anyone:

"I was one who said that which was good, and repeated that which was loved. Never did I say anything evil to a powerful one against any people... I gave bread to the hungry and clothing to the naked. Never did I judge two brothers in such a way that a son was deprived of his inheritance.

"I was one beloved of his father, praised of his mother, whom his brothers and sisters loved."

Which was a nice and most commendable thing to be; and to that ideal of personal behavior, as to the concept of his society as it was "on the first occasion," the Ancient Egyptian clung throughout his long and winding history.

Pharaoh or commoner, he sought consciously to be just, decent, honest and fair; and while he often may not have achieved it, at least the ideal was there, and at least it gave to him some certainty and serenity in a world that was not always as certain and serene as he would have liked it to be.

There are those today, usually young, who make the Egyptian journey with some mystical conviction that here there are secrets that will provide answers to a chaotic and churning world. There are none save those that have always applied, in every time and circumstance: be as good as possible—do the best you can—treat others decently—be fair, be honest, be kind. They are precepts as easy, and as hard, as they have always been.

Behind the eternal smile—confident, knowing, seeming to possess a subtlety it may possess only in the sentimental imaginings of the beholder swayed by the Ancients' insistence—seeming to tremble on the verge of some knowledge it never quite imparts, alive with some secret it never quite discloses—there lies only the confidence of a people who felt with an absolute certainty conferred by the gods that they had found a sensible balance between human nature and the necessities of an orderly and peaceful world.

And so, in the main, they had.

And so, perhaps, they have more right than most to look out upon the centuries, which to them are no more than a passing moment, with a serene and pleasant air.

Photographer's Note

It is a rare opportunity when a photographer is offered the challenge to explore a rich and ancient culture in the company of an author of Allen Drury's stature. My thanks go to him for his faith in my work and for asking me to be part of this memorable venture. Indeed, the experience was a very special one. Through my photographs, I hoped to capture and reveal the unique and timeless mystery of Egypt — at once so tangible and yet so elusive.

I would also like to extend my appreciation and thanks to Tony Palladino who designed this book, to all those individuals in Egypt who helped to make our project possible, and to the Metropolitan Museum of Art for supplying us with a photograph of the statue of Queen Hatshepsut (Rogers Fund and Contribution from Edward S. Harkness, 1929).

Alex Gotfryd